THE ART OF GETTING BACK UP

*9 Simple Steps to Get You Back Up
When Life Knocks You Down*

Wayne Salmans

DEDICATION

This book is dedicated to my wife, Brittany. You have stood beside me through the good and the bad, loved me when I felt unlovable, pushed me when I was playing small, and taught me to enjoy this ride we call life. I love you.

To our kids Gideon, Maddox, Keza, Hudson and Hadley, the greatest joys of my life. You make me proud every day.

To each and every one of us who has ever had a facedown moment and then had the courage to get back up.

You inspire me.

TABLE OF CONTENTS

FORWARD

It was a beautiful, sunny January day in the Adirondack Mountains. I was walking on a snow-covered dirt road east of Old Forge, New York. The sky was deep blue and clear, revealing the rugged mountains that surrounded me. It was a perfect place and time to die.

That was my plan, to end my life. To walk out into the wilderness, find an isolated road, hike into the woods, get drunk, remove all my clothes, fall asleep, and freeze to death. I wouldn't be found until the spring thaw. They might not even know who I was. I had left my car in Syracuse, dumped all my ID's into a trash can, and taken a bus into the mountains. I even hitchhiked the final 26 miles into Old Forge. I didn't want anyone to find me. And, I didn't think anyone would miss me.

As I walked along the road, I began to talk to myself. I would ask questions, and then I would answer. I now believe I had a conversation with God. Maybe it was just my imagination. But, how else would God talk with me? I realized that life and death were an ongoing, eternal cycle in nature. I could see dead limbs and trees, with new growth starting up beside them. In the spring, they would continue their intended growth to maturity. Then, they would die too, and provide nourishment for the next generation.

This internal dialogue (I also spoke much of it out loud) calmed my spirit, and I finally realized that this was not the right plan. I didn't know what I would do, but it wasn't time to die. When I got back to the town, I called my dear friend, Kathy O'Shaughnessy. She got me admitted for psychiatric care at Strong Memorial Hospital in Rochester, New York. A process of healing and growth began.

Amazingly, two months later I was appointed Director of Training for a three-state Region of Century 21. Three years later I became Regional Director and CEO of Century 21 of New York, and just three years after that was asked to take over a four-state Mega Region based out of Dallas, Texas. What an astounding recovery from a suicide attempt!

Ten years after that, things got very dark again. I was fired from my job as C21 Divisional President, I was old (I thought), and not very confident about my prospects. In 1999, I went to an Alcoholics Anonymous meeting in Austin, Texas and declared, "I'm Dave and I'm an alcoholic." I spent the next year recovering from this addiction and from being a smoker. I received amazing support from my boss, Mo Anderson, CEO of Keller Williams Realty International.

Over the next ten years, I helped her grow the company, served as VP and the Dean of Keller Williams University. I co-authored five best-selling books including *The Millionaire Real Estate Agent* (the all-time top-selling book in the real estate industry and still #1 in that category on Amazon).

In 2009, I got hit with a triple whammy: I was asked to leave my high-paying job, my oldest son Bradley died, and I lost the emotional love of my life partner. I was devastated and at a loss about my life. It took me two years of reflection, therapy and mountain biking to get over this. But, in the past seven years, I have co-authored two more books and helped launch another exciting national company (Master Networks) with a young, visionary leader, Chas Wilson. And, I am writing my own memoires: *SEEKER: A Journey Toward Wisdom.* I am happier than I have ever been.

I wish I had Wayne Salmans, and this book, in my life a lot sooner. It would have helped me deal with those downturns and dark times more confidently and quickly. His wisdom is both practical and profound. As a person who has been through the "valley of the shadow," I encourage you to absorb its wisdom before you really need it.

Here is what I know: all high-achievers will deal with failure. They will deal with doubt, discouragement and even depression. They will feel fear and weakness. They will lose friends they thought were forever. They will feel judgment they don't deserve. Their hopes and dreams will get cloudy and unsure. They will want to stop trying so hard. They will want to avoid the pain.

Here is what I also know: this is the path of the free enterprise warrior. This is the story of the entrepreneur. This is the burden of heroic leaders. It comes with the territory. It's part of the game. It's the challenge you must endure. And, beyond the darkness is light. Beyond the pain is joy. Beyond the burden is contribution. Beyond the doubt is meaning.

So, have at it. Bring it on. Get ready. Prepare for it. Absorb the wisdom of *The Art of Getting Back Up*. Learn the steps and master the skills. Feel the power, the resilience, and the tenacity. Bring that confidence to your work, to your venture, to your purpose. Know that you will certainly get knocked down, but you will never stay down. You have the unstoppable power of persistence. You embrace the optimism and challenge of always getting back up. Enjoy the journey.

-- Dave Jenks
Best Selling Author and Co-Author
of *"The Millionaire Real Estate Agent"*

PREFACE

I was laying alone, flat broke, on the cold floor of an empty building in Alaska, in the heart of winter. That was the moment I realized what rock bottom felt like.

The journey to becoming broken is not that unique. Like you, I had worked hard, spent years growing and building myself and my business. My subconscious mind was full of beliefs about how I thought life was supposed to be. How I was supposed to live up to the expectations of myself and everybody else. But I had failed. I had a new reality, and it sucked.

This book is not as much about how I screwed up, as it is about how I got back up. You can, too.

What you hold in your hands is not theory; this is a road map, a guide, a system to getting back on your feet.

When I laid on that floor, homeless and alone, I had the most significant "aha" of my life: "No one is coming to save me." At that moment, I realized one thing. I could end my own life or be my own hero.

Many don't understand the thoughts of suicide, and before that moment, I didn't get it either. In the days leading up to that moment, I got a glimpse of the desperation people experience because that was exactly how I felt.

We live in a world held together in our monkey-like minds by labels and the ability to see everything in polarity, black or white, good or bad, yes or no. We often find our security in this world under those labels. We can be a good parent, good worker, wealthy, respected...yet when those labels disappear, when the money leaves, you feel less than naked.

Not knowing who you are leaves you to wonder, *"Why am I here?"* If you are unable to answer that question or worse, you screwed up and hurt people along the way; you may ask, *"Would everything just be better if I wasn't here? Would the world be a bit happier if I left?"*

In my deciding moment, I thank God that I realized I needed to Be My Own Hero.

Like me, you have the same choice, to be an accidental tourist on this journey of life, or to be a goal-oriented traveler, with the direction and the tools to experience life with intent and purpose. A fully-lived life.

If you're serious about learning how to get back up, about being your own hero, about stepping up instead of stepping out, this book is for you. This is my story, from the very bottom of my heart to yours.

INTRODUCTION:
STEP UP

Everybody has a story. We love parts of our story, especially those scenes where we get to be the good guy, the champion, maybe even the hero. But we also have parts of our story that make us ashamed, dark places where we make stupid mistakes and bad choices, where we hurt ourselves and others, where we fall down and feel like the villain.

I want you to know that I'm in a great place now. I have balance and success in my business, and most importantly in my life. To the best of my abilities, I stay true to my priorities, I love my family and am quick to help others. But the reason I wrote this book has to do with the time in my life where I had no balance, and when everything I valued came tumbling down around me.

When I first wrote my story for this book, I told it like a little tale I had heard. Written from a removed, third-person perspective, starting out "Once upon a time...", skimming over the painful details and failures, and ending with a whispered confession: "That man was me."

But, in order to get up (like we will learn in Step 2), we have to "Get Real." We have to accept where we have been to move forward.

The Story of How I Fell Down

While I was still quite a young man, I enjoyed amazing success. My business was booming and growing. I had a loving wife and adorable children. I was well known and respected in my small town. I put a lot of effort into being involved in community and social events.

Anyone who looked at my life would have said that I had it all. But things didn't add up. The saying "all that glitters is not gold" definitely applied to me.

Underneath my lovely exterior, I had an internal battle raging. Self-doubt, discontent, a huge void. I had been trying to hide these struggles for years, and my façade held for a while, but then things started spinning out of control.

I tried to fill the emptiness within me by working harder, spending more and more time at the office. I tried to find fulfillment other places, but I just felt wanting and more desolate. My actions caused irreparable damage to my relationship with my wife, which in turn hurt my children. Everything began to spiral out of control.

They say things happen slowly then suddenly. For me, this was very true. My ego, insecurities, lack of better planning, fear, self-sabotage, all came to a head. In a matter of two weeks, I lost business partners, friendships, and multimillion-dollar contracts. The money stopped flowing, but the bills kept coming. I went from king of the hill to sleeping on a floor.

When it all came crumbling down, the events actually reaffirmed my feelings of worthlessness that I had felt all along. I had become a self-fulfilling prophecy.

I found myself lying on the floor of a vacant building, broken and crushed. What I realized was that I was exactly where I thought I deserved to be. As I lay on the floor of this building, I prepared for how I would take my own life.

There was a small place to park about 10 miles down the road that had a big ridge overlooking the ocean. I thought, *I'll just make it look like I had an accident in my car and went over the cliff.*

That's how I was going to end my life.

Lying there, I asked myself if there was anything I needed to do before I completed my plan. Perhaps, I was subconsciously procrastinating, waiting for someone to help me. And then I had a life-altering pause. I had one of the greatest moments of clarity I've ever had.

Suddenly, I heard, "No one is coming to save you." The voice was as audible as if someone were sitting right next to me.

It was then I realized with 100 percent certainty that at that moment the only person who could save me, was me. It wasn't that no one cared about me or that no one loved me. It was the clear-cut awareness that I had to choose one of two options.

I could either check out and take my own life, or I could step up and BECOME MY OWN HERO.

I sat there for hours wrestling with that decision. But, finally, I was able to get up and take the first step towards my new purpose for my life.

I wish I could say it was easy and everything got better right after that. But, of course, it wasn't easy, and things didn't just get magically better. However, I will tell you that by choosing to be my own hero, to step up and get back up, my outlook toward those familiar struggles had changed.

Learn How to Get Back Up and Recover Fast

That was my profound FACE DOWN moment. Many of us have had those moments. This book was written to help those people, like you, who want to get back up, to recover *fast* from your crashes. To be your own hero so you can go on to be the hero for others.

I had worked hard all my life to build my business and family, to create an extraordinary life, and yet I realized it was my subconscious mind that was driving the show. The beliefs I held within myself weren't true. I didn't know how to tackle my demons. The combination of it all led me into hitting rock bottom, to having my face-down moment, to feeling completely screwed.

Like most people, we spend our entire lives trying to avoid pain. Most people spend their entire lives thinking, *I want to avoid pain and avoid failure*. The problem with that is that if you spend your whole life trying to avoid pain and failure, then you make the unconscious decision to play small.

We choose to play it safe. We imagine a great life is a life without pain, a life of standing on the shore safe from the storms. Yet, what is the cost?

Compare these two scenes:

Imagine you're working on top of a 10-story building, and you have no harness, no net, nothing. If you were working on the side of this tall building, you would probably be working very slowly and very cautiously, correct? Because you would think *if I make one little misstep, I'm going fall off the building and die.*

In contrast, picture yourself working on the same building, yet you have a harness on this time. You have a safety strap so you know that if you do trip, you may get a little bumped, but you are not going to fall all the way down.

Which one sounds better? Which one would allow you to do your job more effectively, to play all in?

Now, imagine a second scenario where you had a race to run. Of course you want to win, yet along the route were several 10-foot holes. If you fall in one of the holes, you will never be able to get out. You will be stuck forever, never finishing the race. How would you run that race? My guess is you would run that race very consciously, wanting to avoid the pitfalls.

In the same scenario, imagine you are running the same route, but this time you have a magic ladder in your back pocket. It might hurt a little to fall into a hole, but you know you have a way out. How would you run that race? My guess is you would run that race much faster and with more confidence.

On this journey of life, there will be potholes. But knowing when you encountered a pothole/failure, you were able to get back up, would that change how you approach the run of life? If you knew, *If I fall, I have a strategy to get back up, and it won't be the end of my world,* wouldn't you then think, *I can play all in?*

Whether it is the death of a loved one, filing bankruptcy, the loss of a relationship or the pain of hitting rock bottom, the reality is, we're all going to have brutally tough moments of pain. These might be moments completely out of our control, or moments that are partially or fully our fault; but they all hurt.

Brené Brown, a research professor at the University of Houston and the author of four #1 New York Times bestsellers, says we're all going have face-down moments. These are the points in time where you will get beat-up. You will fall down on the mat. You will not know if you're going to be able to get up. You will be disorientated and frustrated. You will be hurting, and yet, in those moments I want to encourage you.

This book is going to empower you to have the energy, the tenacity, and the bravery within yourself to put one knee up underneath you. Then pull that knee up to your chest and begin the process of standing back up.

This book is also about empowering you for the future; to have the confidence to tackle challenges head-on, because you have the tools in place to recover when you fall.

STEP 1

Stop, Drop & Use a Tool

"If you find yourself on fire don't stand up, don't run. Stop, drop and roll, roll, roll the fire out."
~Dick Van Dyke, NFPA PSA 1970's

Years ago, as a young man in my 20's, I attempted to burn off a small field of grass to allow for cleaning and regrowth. I remember starting the fire with a small lighter, turning around to grab my trusty shovel, then looking to back to see the fire take off like a cat after a mouse. Within two minutes, the fire was ten times bigger than I had ever wished for and quickly getting closer and closer to my mother-in-law's very nice home!

I sent my former wife to dash to the house, grab the first fire extinguisher she could find and get back outside as rapidly as possible.

She yelled at me, "How do I use this thing?"

I hollered back "Pull the pin, aim, and squeeze!"

With that, I saw her pull the pin, aim at the nearly barn-sized fire and squeeze. But I had forgotten to convey one very simple, but crucial, part of the instructions: which way to aim. As she pulled the trigger, her entire head was engulfed in white firefighting powder! She made the most surprised shriek I have ever heard, and I knew things had just gone from bad to worse. We did eventually get the fire out and then we spent the next several hours at the ER getting her eyes washed out.

From that moment, I learned two powerful things: 1) I shouldn't be a fire starter, and 2) As important as it is to have the right tools, knowing *how to use them* is equally as important.

Step One: Stop, Drop and Use a tool.

Have you ever seen someone realize they've caught on fire? We've all seen the videos on YouTube or the internet, where a person being singed by flames realizes that they have to get the fire out. What do they do? Obviously, they don't say, "Oh, that's crazy," and then do nothing. If they know what to do, they stop, drop to the ground and then do something to help themselves. They grab a tool. They grab a blanket or whatever else is close to help them to put the fire out.

These nine lessons I am about to share with you are the tools. They are what you will need to use to get back up throughout the course of your life. These are the step you take when you discover something in your life is on fire, or something is not working the way you planned. When that happens, I want you to do the same thing you would do if you were actually on fire: Stop, drop, and use a tool.

Awareness of your reality is the beginning of this process. The first step to getting back up is to realize YOU ARE ON FIRE!

Let's explore this state of "being on fire." This is NOT a good thing. It does not mean you are on a roll; it means the opposite. It is the point when you recognize your situation is not working. When you acknowledge, "I've screwed up." When you admit, "I've hit rock bottom."

Maybe you realize a business transaction has fallen apart and it's not going to come back to life. Maybe a relationship you're in is on a path to nowhere, or it's destined to fail. Being "on fire" is a point in life when your situation needs change NOW.

Jim Rohn says, "You can't change your destination overnight, yet you can get the ship turned around and going in the right direction." Awareness may not get you where you want to go immediately, yet it can get you to at least change your course.

Have you ever been on a road trip and realized you were going in the wrong direction? Every mile you go is another mile that you'll have to travel back. Once, I was driving through Pennsylvania. It was late at night and I missed my turn, so I had to keep going because there was nowhere to turn around. It was crazy. I distinctly remember how I had to drive 15 miles in the wrong direction, knowing that I would just have to turn around and drive those 15 miles back. That meant I was 30 miles behind where I needed to be.

One of the first things successful people realize when they're going the wrong direction is if they spend more time going the wrong direction, they're going to be twice as far off track because they've still got to come all the back as well.

How do you know if you're going in the wrong direction?

How do you know you are "on fire"?

Some people might question, *How do I know when something should end?*

How do I know when I need to stop doing what I'm doing and that my way isn't working?

Sometimes we know in our gut that the decision we have made is the wrong one, yet we want to avoid the pain of the decision we need to make. It may be distressing to stop when things aren't working out.

Thomas Merton presented this concept, "The more you try to avoid suffering, the more you suffer." All too often, we suffer to avoid suffering.

Where in your life are you avoiding a decision because you know it will be tough?

Where are you dodging having a conversation because you don't want to stir the pot or deal with the consequences?

Have you decided instead, to let a situation grow and get worse?

A perfect example of "suffering to avoid suffering" is a bad relationship. Each day sucks more than the last. Still, you keep going because you don't want to experience the pain that comes from ending the relationship. Even though you know eventually it's not going to end well, you let it continue. You are suffering over and over to avoid suffering. You are on fire!

In a business or financial setting, you might keep pushing on a deal that is hitting roadblock after roadblock with no end in sight. It is costing you time and money, but you are afraid of the consequences of just stepping away. You are on fire, and you need to put it out!

Another way of looking at why we suffer is summed up in this question my friend Hank Avink likes to ask, "Do you make decisions or wait until they are made for you?"

As an example, in an office setting we might need to tackle the difficult action of having to fire somebody. One of my coaching clients was a business owner. He needed to let someone on his team go. He had known for a while that this person needed to be gone, and I asked him why he hadn't just made it happen.

He said, "I just don't know how to stop. I just don't know what I need to do." But the reality was, he did know! Every night, he would lay in bed distressed over the negative impact this person was having on his team. He was suffering.

What he didn't realize was, by delaying the firing conversation, he was suffering to avoid suffering.

His business was suffering. His personal life was suffering. All the stress and anxiety caused him pain. His family was suffering because he was too distracted to just relax and enjoy being with them.

So many areas of his life were suffering all in an effort to avoid the suffering of a five or 10-minute conversation with the team member. He was suffering over and over and over to avoid one brief moment of suffering.

The first thing that I want you to explore is: *When do I need to stop?* Is there an area of your life, or a relationship, or a business venture that you know is not going to work and yet, you're suffering to avoid suffering?

Help clarify your answer by applying the following questions:

- What am I holding onto that isn't serving me?

- Has my dream changed to where I now know in my heart it won't end well?

- Where am I suffering to avoid suffering?

When you answer these questions and realize you are on fire: **Stop, drop and then grab a tool!**

Realize that the further you go down a path the more miles you will have to travel back. Chasing a dream that isn't working or holding on to someone that you know is not the person for you is only going to give you a longer road to head back to where you started.

Think about it this way, when you realize that you or someone around you is bleeding, what is the first thing you do? You stop and apply pressure. You stop, drop and you grab a towel or a bandage, then you apply pressure to the cut.

Ask yourself these questions:

- What am I pretending not to know?

- What's not working that I'm pretending is working?

- How long have I tried my current tactic without progress?

- What do I know in my gut that I need to do differently?

- Am I attempting a strategy that's doomed to fail?

- When I know something isn't working, how do I give up?

One of the tough parts in the process is deciding to give up. Even when our strategy is doomed to fail, we have been taught, over and over by so many motivational books and quotes TO NEVER GIVE UP, to have grit and never give up, never give up!!! OK then...*Well, how do I quit?*

The problem with the typical "be strong" approach is sometimes it is time to stop. We are not talking about stopping because it is too hard, or it isn't fun. We are talking about something that is not working. Something that will never be worth what it is costing you.

If your strategy isn't working, you've got to let go of it to move forward. One of the toughest things for us to admit is that a venture or an idea has failed. We don't want to quit because that is FAILURE. Failure to live up to our expectations, failure to impress those watching, failure to meet the needs that you expected to be met. Failure.

As a culture, when did we decide failure was a bad thing? Almost everything we learn in life has a component of failure along the road to success. Say you want to teach a child to tie their shoe. You demonstrate and then talk them through it. Maybe they have some success, but then they try it on their own, and the laces just flop to the side. We don't call them a failure; we tell them to keep practicing.

Practice is really just controlled failure. The problem is, as adults, we turn verbs into nouns. Verbs indicate action; there is motion and continuance. Nouns are static, absolute. When a baby is learning to walk, and they fall, we say "he fell" (verb), not "he is a faller" (noun). As adults, if we fail (verb), we say "I am a failure" (noun).

I'm going to give you some indicators—we'll call them red flags—so you can begin to identify when something is not working, whether it's with a project, a plan, or a relationship. When you have strategies where you check in with yourself before it's too late, you can take steps proactively, rather than being forced into a corner.

Read over the following statements and see if any of them resonate with you.

- My trusted advisors tell me it's the wrong path.

- I keep taking actions, but there are no improvements to my results.

- I am fighting for my idea or venture to work because I don't want others to see it isn't working.

- I am not getting a return on my investment of time, money or energy.

- I realize my path is out of alignment with my true goal.

- Succeeding is more about my ego than the end result.

- I continue taking risks which put my family in harm's way.

- I am pretending not to see the writing on the wall.

Examine your motives. Apply these statements to your situation honestly. If they feel familiar or are spot on, there is a chance you are on fire and need to pull the plug or alter your path.

You might realize you are working hard on getting your plan to work, but it's not going the way you want it to go. It may be time, as the saying goes to "check yourself before you wreck yourself."

Often, getting to the next level or getting to the next stage of your life requires ending something or releasing something. Successful people know when to stop, when to let go, and when to move forward.

One of the most important decisions you'll make in your life is what you're going to *stop doing*, what you're going to *not do,* and then what you're going to *focus on.*

I've found that when we pour our blood, sweat, and tears into a strategy, we are so emotionally and/or financially invested that letting go is very, very painful. Rather than stopping, and admitting it is simply not going to work, we white-knuckle it, and pray for a miracle. The queen of good advice, Ann Landers, wrote, "Some people believe holding on and hanging in there are signs of great strength. However, there are times when it takes much more strength to know when to let go and then do it." The goal is to stop seeing your disappointment in a entirely negative view, but to see it as a diversion on the journey.

Have you ever had the highly frustrating experience of walking up to the front door of your home and realizing the door is locked and your keys are still laying on the counter?

If you are locked out of the house, you've got do something about it. This is something you just can't ignore. You have to deal with it right away.

So, after searching desperately for an open window, or unlocked door, the obvious step is to call a locksmith. It might take hours for them to even get to you. You have to sit there as they work on the door while your groceries melt in the back seat, and on top of all that, you have to pay the locksmith for your suffering.

All of this energy and effort goes into just getting back into your house.

If this has ever happened to you, what did do you do the next day or maybe even that same afternoon? Did you decide "I am never going to let that happen again." Get in your car, drive to Home Depot, get a couple of spare keys, buy a fake rock hide-a-key, drive straight home and place that hide-a-key where you can access it in case you get locked out again. Maybe even give one of the spare keys to the neighbor.

Let's look at your thought process leading up to having the spare key made: I'm never going to let that happen again. I'm never going to be stuck outside of my house for hours, while I wait for somebody to come over and open the door. It took too long. It cost too much. I'm going to come up with a strategy of getting back in the house quicker.

That is your thought process leading up to having the spare key made. When you hide that hide-a-key outside your home, you suddenly have peace of mind, don't you? You might think, *Next time, when I get locked out of the house, I'll have a strategy to get back into the house quickly.*

We take preventative methods all the time in our physical realm. We buy bandages before we need them, we have health insurance, we change the oil in our car. However, we rarely take these actions in our emotional world. See, we experience a failure and it gets us stuck. Or we hit a wall and we spend a ton of energy, effort, and time to get back into our emotional house.

Why don't we, in our mental world, in our emotional world, use hide-a-keys? Why don't we develop a system and outline the steps needed to get back into our home? That's what sharing these steps with you is all about.

First acknowledge, then stop, drop, and grab a tool.

Do you have a hide-a-key?

These are the steps that you can use to get back up. You may tweak them and make them your own. This is the beginning of you not only having hide-a-keys and strategies in your physical world.

It's the beginning of you having hide-a-keys and strategies in your mental world, too. We want to be prepared, and a have a plan for bouncing back because the amount of time it takes a person to get back up is a defining factor in life.

One of my favorite things to tell my clients is, "Successful people are able to get back up quickly."

Imagine you own a professional hockey team (just in case you didn't know, I'm a die-hard hockey fan), and an amazing player comes to your team. He's incredible, but for every two-minute shift on the ice, it takes him 30 minutes to recover, which means, at the most he his playing two or three shifts per game when the average player plays 24 shifts per game.

If that were the case, he would never stay on your team. Even if he were incredible in those two minutes, if it took him 30 minutes to get back up, to recover, you would fire the dude. His recovery time would just be too long.

Successful people have strategies. They're able to recover quickly, so ask yourself: *How fast do I recover?* Unsuccessful people will stay down forever. Successful people recuperate quickly. What I want you to begin thinking about is, *How do I recover faster?*

I'm not talking about never falling down. You want to be prepared; hide the key, develop strategies to get back up quickly, recover faster, and return to the ice before anybody else.

Have a check-yourself-before-you-wreck-yourself tool.

After having my first marriage fall apart, I am very careful to stay on track and in-tune in this second opportunity I have been given. One of the things I do with my wife every Sunday is sit down and ask her questions like:

- "How are we doing?

- "On a scale of 1-10, where are we at?"

- "What do you love that I do?"

- "What do you want me to never stop doing and what would you love me to stop doing?"

- Then I ask her, "What's one great way I can support you this week?"

I check in with our relationship regularly, before it's too late.

As I learned early in my life, things happen slowly and then suddenly. We drift away from our spouses if we're not careful, if we don't have a strategy and a way to check ourselves.

Have a methodical system. Every week, check in with the people and things that are important to you, including yourself. Your answers to the following questions are excellent indicators of how you are doing. They also serve as red flags if your life has gotten off-track.

How am I feeling? Am I stressed out? Do I have unexplained anger building up within me? Am I beginning to pull away from relationships? Am I beginning to pull away from friendships? Am I beginning to go into isolation?

When I was on my way to rock bottom, I pulled away from everyone. I knew what I was doing, and yet I didn't stop myself long enough to realize *why* I was doing it.

One of the things that will allow you to enjoy this journey a little bit more is when you have the awareness to ask yourself the tough questions. *What's working? What's not working? What am I pretending not to know?*

Then understanding sometimes you just need to stop. You need to evaluate what's working. You need to tool up. Maybe you need a new strategy. Maybe you need to approach what you are doing from a different angle.

Consciously checking in with where you are at on a consistent basis can make a huge difference. It can be a game changer.

Step One. Acknowledge. Then stop, drop, grab a tool.

Consistently check in with yourself in a way that allows you to do so before it's too late. At the end of this book, the last step I'm going to give you contains several different strategies to check yourself before you wreck yourself. For now, you can begin by checking in with yourself once a week.

Am I stressed? Am I angry? Am I frustrated? Am I isolating myself? Am I building up resentment?

All right, my friends, we have tackled the first step. Let's keep going.

STEP 2

Get Real

*"The pessimist complains about the wind; the optimist
expects it to change; the realist adjusts the sails."*
~William Arthur Ward

*"You do what you can for as long as you can, and when you
finally can't, you do the next best thing. You back up but you
don't give up.*
~Chuck Yeager

It's winter in Alaska and it's cold, really cold. Like freeze-your-nose-hairs, -20 degrees kind of cold. Foot after foot of snow is falling. The harshness of the cold outside is beginning to work its way inside the vacant building where I am sleeping.

My mind is anything but cold. No, it is red hot with self-loathing thoughts. I have thoughts like, *You've failed. This is over. You'll never recover. You're stupid. You're worthless. This is the end of the world. You'll never be able to come back from this.*

Over and over these thoughts spin inside my head like a helmet of thorns, crushing into my mind.

When I realized how extreme my thoughts really were, it was a huge wake-up call, and my vision began to clear.

This is Step 2. Get Real.

When you hear yourself talking in extremes, it's that inner critic or that judge in your mind within you telling you the worst of the worst. *This is the worst thing that could ever happen to me and there's no recovering from it.*

Yet, here's what's interesting about these messages we tell ourselves: THEY ARE NOT TRUE!!!

You've got to Get Real. You have to ask yourself, *Is this really the worst-case scenario?* Yes, a transaction may have fallen apart. Yes, a relationship may have ended. Yes, you might have screwed up. But is it really the end of the world?

Here's what I want you to realize: most people, especially high achievers, have blind spots. (If you're reading this I am assuming that you're a high achiever, you're someone who is passionate about living your full purpose and being all that you can be).

These blind spots manifest themselves in two main ways: we either make things out as really terrible and see them as the worst they can ever be, or we pretend what's happening doesn't matter, like it's not a big deal when there is actually something we need to deal with. You've seen this happen, or most likely you've also done this yourself.

For example, look at Matty in the fourth grade. He got an F on a spelling test. So he tells himself, *I got an F on a test. That means I'm stupid. That means my teachers won't like me; my parents won't believe me. That means I probably won't be able to go to college, and that means I probably won't be able to get a good job, which means no one will want to marry me. And so, I will never have kids. I will probably die alone. This means my life is probably over.*

We've all had conversations like this in our heads.

If a realtor has a transaction fall apart, she might think, *This proves I'm terrible at this job, that I shouldn't even be in this business. You know what? No one will probably hire me. I don't even know what I'm going to do with my life. I'm just a failure.*

What the %^$#!? It was one transaction! It was one F on the test! Yet, some days we make things as extreme as they can be. You've got to take a breath, get perspective and get real.

On the other side of this coin, where a lot of you may fall, is that we can sometimes decide an occurrence is so tiny in importance, that we pretend it doesn't matter. We wear rose-colored glasses.

Remember *Monty Python and the Holy Grail*, where the Black Knight is guarding the footbridge and as King Arthur attempts to cross the bridge, a battle ensues? King Arthur continues to swing at the Black Knight, removing one limb at a time with each swipe. Meanwhile, the Black Knight asserts repeatedly, "I'm fine! It's nothing but a flesh wound!" Clearly the dude has major wounds. He's lost his legs and his arms!

It is fascinating that as high achievers, we sometimes will experience pain or failure and in an effort to not be a victim, we might say, "I'm good, I'm fine. It's nothing. I'm totally okay." But when you do that, you are stealing from yourself the opportunity to learn from what has happened.

Tony Robbins expressed this thought well in this paraphrase, "No one should go into their garden and chant, 'There are no weeds. There are no weeds. There are no weeds.' For people to be true leaders, they have to first see things as they are, not worse. Then see that it can better than it is, and then make it better."

Choosing not to get real and process the pain will usually cause more significant pain. If you don't get real with what's going on now, this discomfort will probably show up later in life. If you don't get real about the fact that your wound hurts, or that you've actually experienced a misstep, you'll pay the price later.

Leading up to the moment where I almost took my life, I didn't have these steps. In hindsight, one of the questions I should have asked myself was, *If I was looking at someone else, what would I be saying?* Would I tell them "Your life is over," or "This is the end?" No. I'd say, "Yeah, this sucks" to let them know I understood. And yet here's the reality. A lot of people have been through a lot of pain and misery, and they have gotten back up. Deep within me, I knew this and as my epiphany rolled over me, I began to ask myself some powerful questions.

The questions were: *Is this really the end or could I recover? Could I be okay? Maybe it's not tomorrow, yet in five years could I recover? What about ten years? If it is possible to get back up at some point should I give up now?*

I remember thinking at that moment among other things, *You are six figures plus in debt. How are you ever going to recover?* But then one of the thoughts in the back of my mind was, *You know what? If I were making $2 million a year, this wouldn't be that big of a deal. Could I make $2 million?* I could.

I asked myself, *If I had 100 years to recover, could I do it?* And I knew I could. *Well, what if I only had 50 years, could I recover?* Probably. *What if I only had 20 years?* Yeah, I could recover in 20 years. *What if I only had five?*

I began to realize that if I got real with what was going on, I could recover. I could get back up. I could put another deal together. I could find another great relationship, and my life could improve. But before I started to think about what my life might look like, I had to get real first. This wasn't the end of the world, and yet what I was going through was also not nothing. I had to start where I was.

There is a formula that behavioral psychologist Bruce Tuckman came up with years ago, called Forming, Storming, Norming and Performing. He built the formula mostly around team projects, and yet I think it applies to our lives.

Every day, we encounter new challenges and new opportunities; we continually go through these four phases.

Something new or unexpected happens, triggering the New Form, that throws us into a mental Storm. But eventually we will come to terms with the new scenario—that's Norming. When we get to that place, it allows us to then get into action, to move forward and that stage is called Performing.

Tuckman said, "In your life, you're going to experience many new Forms." Say you walk into a group and you need to find a place to sit. You walk in, and you say, "Hey, I've never been in this building before," or "The chairs are different." Whatever you happen to say or notice, you will go through a Forming process. You'll say, "Things are different," and when you do, that will throw you into a Storm.

The Storm is: What's going on? Where should I sit? Do I know anybody? What's happening? The new environment throws you into a Storm.

At some point you will reach the point where you will say, "You know what? It is what it is. I'll sit there." That's the Norming phase: realizing your situation is what it is. *Here's what's going on, I'm willing to accept it.*

Which moved you into Performing. And you grab a chair and sit down.

Here's how it applies to a relationship. Let's say you have a relationship that falls apart. That's a new Form in your life. You thought it was going to last forever, but then it ends. That's a new Form, causing you to go into a Storm, and the Storm feels like, "Damn, what's going on?" It throws you into a whirlwind, where you will ask yourself, *What am I going to do? Am I going to be okay?*

At some point after a change, during this second phase, most people come to a place of acknowledgment. *I'm in a Storm. My* relationship has fallen apart, and there's nothing I can do to repair it. Only then, after this realization, can you get into Norming; *It is what it is.* Once you are there, then you can progress into Performing and taking the next action you need to take.

In business, let's say you have a transaction put together and it's beautiful, and then the whole thing falls apart. Well, that's a new form, that's a new state of being. So, the transaction falling apart, causes you to go into a Storm. You question, *What could I have done differently? Why did I let this happen? Will people stop trusting me? How am I going to pay the bills?*

After you have accepted the new state, then you will realize, *The transaction fell apart. There's nothing I can do about it.* You'll get back up, and that's Norming. After you have gone through those stages, then you can take action, and start putting together your next transaction.

Here's what I want you to remember. A lot of people in life get stuck in the Storm.

Have you ever talked to someone who said, "When my divorce happened it ruined my life, and I don't think I'll ever recover."? You feel sad for them and might respond with, "Wow, that sounds really terrible. When did that happen?" And their answer shocks you: "1973."

Taken aback you'd sit there and wonder, *Are you freaking kidding? You need to go watch Frozen and "Let it go." Man, do you ever need to move on.*

Some people get stuck in the Storm, not for days, not for weeks; people have gotten stuck in the Storm for way longer than they should.

They have a new Form: they go through a divorce, a bankruptcy or the loss of a business. They get in that storm and don't know how to get out. And then they let themselves become a victim and stay in that Storm for years and years and years.

Still, there are other people, who recognize: *There's a new Form. Yeah, it's frustrating, but it is what it is. I'm going to get real about it. I'm not going to make it worse than it has to be. I'm not going to pretend like it's nothing. I'm going to evaluate it for what it is, and I will be able to get into Norming. Then I can take action and move forward into Performing, the next phase.*

One of the differences between successful people and unsuccessful people is their ability to get real and move through the Storm.

Forming happens with professional athletes all day long.

I recently interviewed a professional NFL wide receiver and asked him, "How to do you get back up? How do you emotionally recover when you miss that game-winning catch or fumble the ball when your whole team is counting on you?" His response was beautiful. He looked me dead in the eye and simply said, "I learned to dust it off and get right back up. I learned to have a short memory." Once he moved into Performing, he could go and make the next play without being distracted by the failure of the previous play.

In the 1940's running a four-minute mile was impossible. Doctors stated if you ran a four-minute mile, you would die. Legend stated it was simply impossible; humans had been trying for thousands of years to achieve that goal and even when chased by angry bulls no one had run faster than the current record, which at that time was 4:01.

Then the impossible happened. Somebody did it! Roger Bannister broke the four-minute barrier, running four miles in 3:59.4. That caused a new Form in the entire sport. It threw all the other runners into a Storm of, "How's that possible?", "That's crazy." and then, "Could I do that?"

The great runners said, "It's obviously possible, and yet I've got to change." They went from the Form—*somebody did it*—into a Storm—*how's that even possible?* They said, "You know what? Well, if he did it, I must be able to do it. I've got to grow into someone I haven't been before. I've got to do things differently." That's the Norming part, the acceptance. They got real, which allows them to get into Performing. In the next decade, more and more runners ran sub 4-minute miles.

Here's a fantastic story: In 2017, Nike put out a challenge. They took three of the top marathon runners in the world and told them, "We're going to do something that's never been done before. You're going to run a marathon in less than two hours." Never been done before. Do you think that caused them to go into a Storm? "This is impossible." There's the Storm. "How do we even do this?" They were given all new shoes and gear. But here's the exciting part. They did it in two hours and less than a minute. *So close!*

This is what's cool about the challenge for these runners. They're going to have to go through a new Form. They know that it can be done, and yet they're going to have to adjust, and I guarantee you that it will happen. The new Form of this is possible. *How the heck do we do this? I've got to adjust, I've got to change and then we've got accomplish it.*

I see this happen with leaders frequently. A leader is thrown into a new Form, where they realize if they want to go to the next level, they're going to have to change. They're going to have to adjust their leadership style. They're going to have to raise their skills. They're going to have gone from being just a manager to being a real leader. They're going to have to start asking more questions so they can have success with the people who they are leading.

When they have an awareness of, *I'm going to change*, that's the Form that throws them into the Storm of *How do I do this? What do I do? Is it worth it?* They see a different experience and will eventually say, *You know what? It is worth it. I'm going to do it.* Then they accept it. They get real. It's at that point that they can Perform.

Here's the reality for all of us. What got you here probably isn't going to get you where you want to go. When you are ready to grow, you're going to have to get real and acknowledge that, *I'm going to have to go through a Storm. I'm going to have to grow into a higher version of myself if I want to continue down this path of leadership, down this path of being all I can be.*

So, here's my challenge to you. Get real. Accept your life and situation for what they are. Don't view it as worse than it really is, but also, don't make it nothing; accept it.

Realize there is a new Form in your life. Decide to go through the Storm. The reality is there's no way around the Storm. You have to go through the Storm. You can't go over it, you can't go under it, you can't go around it, you've got to go through the Storm, whatever it is. You've got to go through the challenge.

If you want to be the biggest bodybuilder in the world, you've got to go through a whole lot of work to get there. There's no easy way. When you go right through the Storm, only then, can you grow into a new person and Perform on a higher level.

If you're going to impact the world, and you've got a Storm brewing up before you, you've got to get real first. Then you can get through the Storm. Make the choice. Be brave. Get real. Go through the Storm, to the other side.

I BELIEVE IN YOU! And I know that you've got this. Make the decision to be all that you can be. Decide there is a new Form and that you are the person who can bust through.

Say, *I'm the person brave enough to get real with myself. I'm the person fearless enough to say, "I screwed up and I'm going to learn the lesson. I'm going to grow into a person I haven't been before. I'm going to get through the Storm. I'm going to grow into a whole new version, so I can help others by helping myself."*

STEP 3

Two Roads

"Two roads diverged in wood and I, I took the one less traveled by. And that has made all the difference."
~Robert Frost"

"Negative emotions are a sign that something is going unaddressed. They are a call to action. Positive emotions are the reward for taking the correct action."
~The Subtle Art of not giving a F*ck

Step Three: Acknowledge That You Have Two Roads.

Several years ago, I met a man named Nick Vujicic at a real estate convention. Nick was one of the guest speakers and distinctly unique individual. Right off the bat when you meet Nick, you notice something very obvious. Nick has no arms and no legs. You have probably seen his videos online.

His story, telling about the trials he has gone through, was awe inspiring. Yet, what really stood out to me, was when I came back to the hotel that night, and I saw Nick, no arms, no legs, swimming in the pool. I still have no idea how he did it. There's was just a dude in the pool, swimming laps back and forth, something that should have been completely impossible, and yet he was doing it. I can barely swim *with* arms and legs. I remember looking at him and going, "That's incredible."

This is a man who has chosen an extraordinary path. He had a harsh reality, and yet he chose to take the road that led to where I saw him that day.

Step three is acknowledging you have two paths, two different journeys you can choose; it's acknowledging that you're going to have limitations. You're going to have events happen in your life. You're going to have failure in your life, and yet, you've got one of two choices: you can either be the victim, or you can be the victor. You can either be cursed by the limitation, or you can find the blessing in the limitation. All of us make that choice.

Nick was born with no arms and no legs. It would have been incredibly easy for a person in his situation or a similar one to say, "You know what? I have no arms. I have no legs. My life is over. I've been cursed. I'm never going to have an incredible future."

Instead, Nick made the decision we can all make; *I have a choice. I can either be a victim, or I can make something great out of my life, out of my situation.* When you look at his life now, you can't help but be captivated by how amazing he is and that he is living a wonderful life. He has a great wife and a beautiful family. He made a choice not to be a victim, but to be a victor.

A person could put all those limitations on themselves and then spend the rest of their life in that victim state, in the victim cul-de-sac. People like cul-de-sacs. They are a great place to live, they are safe, not too many strangers pass by, and no one is going very fast. But if you are trying to get somewhere, you have to leave the cul-de-sac. You have to find a road.

Victims blame other people. Victims say, "This is everybody else's fault." Victims say, "I can't do what I want to do because of this, this, and this."

Victors say, "What *can* I do? Is there potentially a gift in my limitations?"

When I look at myself, I can see my limitations. I'm not great at the details. I'm not amazing at writing. I struggle with that. I struggle with some of the finer details of business, and this became clear to me when I was in real estate. Yet, there was a blessing in that. Because I wasn't good in that area, I was forced to get help. I was forced to bring people into my life to help me with those parts of the business.

Because I wasn't able to work in those areas effectively, I didn't do it waste time in those activities. Instead I found someone who could do it well. The blessing was, I then went and focused on all the stuff that I was good at. There's a gift to be recognized in the curse.

As a child, I was labeled with ADD and dyslexia and a few other labels. And yet, my dyslexia, my learning disabilities, and my other labels didn't hold me back. Instead, they forced me to become very creative. My flaws and so-called limitations forced me to do things in a way that other people couldn't.

Nowadays it's fascinating; I'm one of the best Scrabble players you will ever meet. It took me years to figure out why, and I wondered, "How am I good at Scrabble when I can't spell to save my life?" I realized my whole life; I've had to be inventive when it came to spelling. I used to continually challenge myself, *Okay. What word can I spell? I'll use that one.* Doing so fostered creativity within me.

All the labels that were put on me as a child have helped me to have an appreciation for other people and their circumstances. It has helped me to care for other people who also have special classifications placed upon them.

It would be so easy to say; *I'm never going to be great because I've got this (whatever this is).* It would be so easy to try to justify, *Because of this failure, I'm never going to be able to do great things.* And yet, the victor, says, *This is simply a moment on my journey. There's probably an opportunity or a great lesson in this experience.*

What do great people do? They realize in every problem there is an opportunity. There's always something great if you choose to learn the lesson. If you choose not to turn down Victim Lane, which just ends in that little cul-de-sac. Instead, choose to be a victor, learn the lessons, then move forward.

Carlos Castaneda phrased this clearly in *The Journey to Ixtlan*, when he said, "We either make ourselves miserable, or we make ourselves strong. The amount of work is the same."

Now, here's what this mindset requires. It takes, not only seeing the limitations as an opportunity but also assuming full responsibility for your life.

As my great friend John Reinhart says, "Your limitations, your failures, will either become your stumbling blocks, and the excuse for your failure or they will become the building blocks that will build a stairway to your success."

You get to make the choice. That's your power. At the end of the day, no matter what happens, you get to make the choice: *Am I the victim, or am I the victor?*

Now, let's discuss the blunt reality. One of the reasons why people resist being the victor is because being the victor requires taking responsibility. It requires owning up to your part in the situation.

Even if it is a situation out of our control, that happened to us, we almost always have a piece in owning responsibility. We can choose how we respond, right?

I love this quote from Sigmund Freud, "Most people do not really want freedom, because freedom involves, responsibility, and most people are frightened of responsibility." The true price of happiness is you taking full responsibility for your life.

If I'm blaming other people, if I say, "They did this, and they did that." Or, if I say, "I would be happy if they did this," or, "I'd be happy when...." Then I'm giving them all my power. I can only be truly happy when I accept full responsibility, when I declare, "Here's what I've been dealt. Here are the cards I have. Whether somebody dealt them to me, or whether they were my choices. I am able to make the choice on what I do with them. I've got to take 100 percent responsibility for my life."

So, the bad news is, if you're somewhere you don't want to be, and you apply this concept, then you own the situation. When you accept that, the good news is, you're the one who can do something about your reality. You don't have to wait around for someone else to fix the problem. You have already claimed responsibility, so you are primed to make it better. Make no mistake, the true price of happiness is full responsibility.

Let's take this one step further. Can you take responsibility, and yet still be in victim mode? The answer is yes, but there is nothing healthy about that state either. One of the great things about many high achievers is that we know we hold the bag, we know we are answerable to the situation we are in. When we make a mistake or have a failure, we pronounce: "I cannot believe I did that." We attempt to be different in this way. Yet, the reality is, sometimes as high achievers, we just beat the crap out of ourselves.

In *The Subtle Art of Not Giving a F*ck*, Mark Manson states, "A lot of people hesitate to take responsibility for their problems because they believe that to be responsible for your problems is also to be a fault for your problems." He also said, "This is not true. We are responsible for experiences that aren't our fault all the time. This is part of life."

When I was at my lowest, I was choosing to stay in victim mode. By doing that I was mistreating and disabling myself. It made sense to me at the time. I knew that I had failed. Failure had not just hurt me; it hurt other people. The impact was broad. I began to rough myself up and say, *I can't believe you did this*, and *Why did you do that?* I went on and on. *You're a terrible dad. You're a failure.* All of this self-loathing.

It took me almost two years after my fall, to realize that beating myself up, over and over and over, didn't help anybody. Beating myself up, putting myself through intense purgatory, wasn't making anything better. It was wasted time. I was behaving like a victim, even though at the same time I thought I was taking responsibility. But I wasn't taking steps to get out of martyr mode.

If you keep beating yourself up, don't take a different action, and don't take any steps forward, you're just a fancy victim. There are so many people that I work with who say, "Oh, I know I should do this. I know I should do that." They think they're taking responsibility, but the reality is, even if they aren't bashing themselves, they're really playing the victim.

I was the only one getting something out of my internal thrashing. I felt good beating myself up because I thought I deserved to be abused. It actually felt right when I was mentally beating the crap out of myself, because I thought that would somehow atone for what I had done. That it would somehow make things better for other people. But then I realized I was being a fancy victim. The moment I realized I wasn't helping any of the people that I said I cared about, was the moment I made the switch to stop being a victim.

Ask yourself these questions: *What are three reasons that would provoke you to stand up out of that puddle, to push yourself off of the mat, after you've gotten knocked down? What are some of the things you're going to fight for?* **Write down the reasons why you are going to get back up.**

For me, one of the biggest reasons to get back up was my kids. I realized that they would be hurt if I stayed down. The benefit to my children was showing them that you can fail and get back up. You can recover. You can be a resourceful person, and just because you screwed up doesn't mean you're a screw-up. I went on a mission to show them that if I can get back up, they can too.

When I started my company, The Hero Nation, I created our creed to remind myself and others of our reason to get up every day:

> "I will become my own hero because;
> My soul demands it,
> my family deserves it,
> and the world is starved for it."

What are your three reasons why you're going to get up out of that mud puddle of self-pity and make the next choice?

Realize you have three essential assets which you can use to lift yourself beyond the victim phase. These are your time, your energy, and your money. These three things are precious commodities, and you get to choose how you spend them.

You are going to spend or invest your time one way or the other. Time is marching on. You cannot stop it.

Victims see a wound and spend their time watching it and waiting for it to get worse. Victors say, "I have a wound, and I should repair it. I should take the steps necessary to heal it. I should take care of it."

Physically you don't want to spend any time ignoring a wound. You could turn into one of those people who have a little cut on their leg, and then a month later, you learn they lost the limb to gangrene.

All too often they have not been giving the wound the attention it needed, or worse, they were ignoring the wound altogether. Conversely, you want to say, "I have a wound, and right now I can fix it before it becomes even bigger." Now, let's apply the same reasoning to other vital parts of your life.

In a work setting, if there is a problem, don't spend time ignoring it. Tackle it head on and fix it. Make sure you're spending your time right. Do the most important things. Make sure you spend your time with the most important people you can. At the end of the day, you can feel good about yourself and say, "I spent my time doing the most important things. I wisely invested my time."

The same goes for a relationship. If something isn't right, you could spend time stewing about the problem, or you could take steps to make it better. Perhaps a friend accused you of not valuing them. You could spend time stewing about their comment, or you could make a plan and take action.

Time and energy are often overlapping. Energy usually involves time. When you look at your energy, you get to choose where to invest that energy. Are you going to spend it wisely, or are you going to waste it?

Imagine you have a paint bucket that you spill in one little corner of a room. You have a choice. Either you can pick up that paint bucket and clean up the mess, or you can say, "I can't believe

I dropped that paint bucket." You can freak out, because you lost that paint, right? You can flail about and throw the paint all over the room in frustration and anger. You can either spend your energy cleaning up the small mess, or you can be a victim and spend your energy making an even bigger mess.

You get to choose what to do, and that flows into time. How you spend your time is going to be the critical difference between being a victim and a victor. Your time is such a precious commodity. Spend it wisely.

The third resource is your money. Money is great if you tell it what to do. If you don't tell it what to do, it will disappear. I want you to sit down and look at your financial situation. Look at the whole picture and ask yourself, *Where can I stop spending money?*

Review your expenses. If you are struggling, cut all non-critical expenses from your budget. Evaluate everything that's going out. A lot of people will spend a lot of money to try to make the pain go away, to try to ignore hurt.

Be intentional about where you spend your energy, where you spend your time, and where you spend your money. Ask yourself these three questions as you consider investing or spending any of the three:

1. Is it in alignment with my goals?

2. Am I getting a high return?

3. Should I spend it somewhere else?

You can't change the past, yet you can make a choice to be a victor and dramatically impact the future. The reality is, you have greatness within you. This is your moment. You've made the decision. You can say, "I'm not going to be a victim. I'm going to step up and be a victor."

STEP 4

Feel the Pain

*"Life without problems is not worth living. What if problems
are the path to ultimate happiness?"*
~WS

"Happiness is found in solving problems, not avoiding them."
*~The Subtle Art of Not Giving a F*ck*

I was 17 years old, and we were driving down old dirt roads in a hot, arid, desert part of Guatemala. The busses slowed as our volunteer mission group full of doctors and nurses pulled up to a dilapidated building serving as the church and a temporary hospital. We unloaded boxes from the back of the vans and laid out the medical supplies inside. I was assigned to take a box and place bottles of some sort of medical ointment on a large wooden table.

I put out the containers as everybody else set up in their stations. Moments later, the people entered for treatment.

Some people had their teeth looked at. Other people had procedures done for their eyes. While all these different activities were taking place, people also came to our table. They were moving slowly. As I looked into their eyes, they seemed sad but glanced at the doctor with hopefulness. The doctor examined the men and women and gave many of them the small bottles of ointment.

I didn't understand the Spanish conversations, so in English I asked him, "These people seem desperate for this lotion. What is it for?" He replied, "It's to treat their leprosy. It will actually cure it. Within about a week, they won't be contagious anymore, and within a couple of months, their disease will completely go away."

I had never understood or been around leprosy before. We don't really experience that disease in the States. The only thing I'd ever heard about leprosy was from the Bible. Basically, I knew that it was bad.

The doctor told me that most people don't die from leprosy. Leprosy begins to affect the skin, and then it kills the nerves. People die because they lose feeling in parts of their bodies, and then because of that, they don't notice injuries. So, someone with leprosy in the leg can run into a door jamb and not realize that they've hurt themselves. They can step on a nail and not realize that they have a wound. When they have wounds, those can turn into infections, and sometimes they will lose their leg or their arm, for example.

What registered in my head was the fact that these people were coming to the clinic in an effort to experience pain again. They wanted to cure their leprosy, so they could literally feel pain. They might not have looked at it that way, but it was exactly what they were seeking.

This blew my mind. Most people spend their entire lives doing everything they can not to feel pain. We treat pain as if it's this terrible enemy that we should run from. In this situation, it dawned on me, that pain is a gift. Without pain, we don't know what to fix. Pain can be one of the greatest gifts in our lives.

That's why Step 4 is: Feel the Pain.

I want you to acknowledge the pain. I want you to feel the pain. Choose to understand that pain is a necessary part of the process and a gift, that if you didn't experience pain, it would actually be a detriment to you.

But here's the catch: as high achievers, too often we ignore the pain. We want to say, "I'm good." We desire to brush it off and simply move forward. We think pain slows us down, yet if we don't deal with pain in the moment, we'll probably have to deal with it later on. If we don't accept it and deal with it now, it'll probably show up later on in our lives.

When you experience failure, or when you experience the loss of a relationship, for instance, I'm going to ask you to feel the pain, accept it, find the gift that's in it and then move forward.

If you get a cut on your arm, don't ignore it. Don't pretend that you don't have a gaping wound. The longer you wait to treat it, the more infected it will get, the bigger of an issue it's going to become.

I once heard the story about a man who had fallen and his leg really hurt. What he didn't know was that he had actually severed his quadricep. He ignored the pain. He had difficulty walking, but he didn't want to go to the doctor. One day, because of the weakness in his leg, he fell down the stairs, and severed the other quad! When he tried to get up, he no longer had any capability to do such a thing. Meanwhile, because of the original injury, his muscle had atrophied up into his leg. He now needed surgery on both legs, and he ended up being in a wheelchair for six months.

When you have a huge cut in your arm or in your heart, let's take care of it. Let's feel the pain, and let's go through it, so we don't have to deal with it later on.

There's a process to moving forward. This is where you can choose to slow down so you can speed up later. It's the experience of going from hitting rock bottom to getting back up or losing everything to recovering.

When life doesn't live up to our expectations, it often causes grief, which manifests in the same way as pain. When people grieve, usually, there are five phases of grief. Sometimes these are really extreme events, and other times, we can go through them quickly. As we work our way through pain or grief, almost all of us will experience these five phases: denial, anger, bargaining, depression, and acceptance. This is a well-known concept, but it is important to take the time and apply it to yourself.

Stage 1 Denial: Pretending it didn't happen in the first place.

Stage 2 Anger: Taking the time to blame other people or blame the situation.

Stage 3 Regret: In the bargaining phase, you might say, "If I would've just done this..." Or, "I could've done this." Or, "Why didn't I do (whatever it was)?"

Stage 4 Depression: Wallowing in victim mode. This stage is close to acceptance, but you are not ready to move forward yet.

Stage 5 Acceptance: This is the stage when you are ready to do what needs to be done to get out of the situation and move forward.

Now, you don't always go through all five phases in that order, and sometimes you may stay in one stage longer than another. It's helpful to understand that when you experience pain when your life goes off the tracks, and a part of it stops working, you may go through those five stages of grieving. That's okay. What's not okay is pretending that everything is alright, while not treating your gaping wound.

So, what the heck do you do?!?! I will walk you through some of the healthy options you can use to feel the pain and then move forward in each one of these stages. Maybe you're trying to handle the loss of a business deal. You will probably go through some of these stages of grief. You may experience denial or isolation, or pull yourself away. Maybe you'll feel anger at yourself, others, God, or the universe; whatever it is. You're angry.

You may go into the bargaining stage. Sometimes, you may sink into depressions on some level. But at the end is acceptance, and that allows you to move forward. I'm going to give you some powerful questions you can ask yourselves and options you can take to feel the pain and then move forward.

The first and most important question to ask yourself is: *What am I feeling?*

Maybe you're feeling sad because life didn't live up to your expectations. Perhaps you thought you were in a forever relationship and it turned out that it wasn't. When life doesn't live up to our expectations, the natural result is sadness. Maybe you're feeling hurt because somebody stabbed you in the back. Maybe someone close bruised you. I want you to consider that it's okay to feel hurt.

Like I mentioned earlier, many of us deny ourselves the ability or a moment to feel pain. The same thing applies to fear. Maybe somebody else hurt you, or possibly you hurt yourself. When this happens, fear might jump up and bite you. When we go through failure or the loss of somebody we love, it can cause distress and anxiety in our lives.

We might get cold feet when we think about the future because we are afraid history will just repeat itself. Our anxiety causes doubt and fear in our own ability to make choices. So, the first question you should just ask yourself is simply: *What am I feeling?*"

Allow yourself to come to terms with whatever it is you fear. There are no right or wrong feelings. Just allow yourself to make the choice and to acknowledge what it really is that you're experiencing. Feel the pain.

YEP, it's okay to feel the pain. Reminds me of that scene from *The Lion King* years ago, when Simba is talking to Rafiki and says, "I can't go back. I've been running away for so long. I've experienced so much pain already."

Rafiki hits Simba on the head with his stick and Simba responds, "Why did you do that?" Rafiki says, "Don't worry about it. It's in the past."

Simba: "Yeah, but it still hurts."

Rafiki: "The past can hurt."

You can either run from it, or you can learn from it. You can always make the choice to feel the pain and learn from it.

The second question to ask yourself has two parts, *What would I have to believe to feel this way?* AND *What else could this mean?*

This is a profound question that may take a minute to soak in, but when it does, it can be incredibly powerful and life-changing.

For example, have you heard someone say as their relationship ends, "That's it! I'm never going to be in another relationship ever again. I'm just not cut out for this relationship thing."? What do they believe to feel this way? Do they think that they aren't capable of loving? Do they believe that relationships never work? Or could it mean that they didn't put their all into the partnership? Or that they just weren't a good match?

Or, in the business world, have you seen a transaction fall apart and then heard the person who lost the business say, "See? I've got to get out of this business. I'm terrible at it." Do they really believe that they aren't good at business? That they aren't capable of doing the work? Or could it be that outside influences caused the deal to fall apart?

What we experience is almost always a result of our interpretation of the event, in other words, the story we make up. And man, does our mind like to make up stories! Sometimes we are fast thinkers and quick to make up stories without taking the time to consider if the story we just made up is 100% true, even when it applies to ourselves.

We have all messed up and then stated, "I'm just a stupid person." Do we really believe we are dumb? Or could it be that we weren't paying attention? Or maybe we hadn't known all the factors in the situation?

Many of these stories we create in our mind are not 100% true, yet we continue to state them over and over. Then, after years of repeating the same stories, they eventually become full-blown "truths" in our mind. We begin to believe what we say over and over even though it may be false.

Acknowledge that we make up stories and that we need to be careful about the stories we make up, too.

Feel the pain and ask yourself these questions:

- What am I feeling?
- What would I have to believe to feel this way?
- What else could this mean?
- Could I choose a different meaning for this?
- What could I learn from this?
- What am I choosing to feel now?

- How would I like to feel?

- What am I willing to do about this right now?

The next action towards reaching the stage of acceptance is forgiveness, and it takes courage.

"Courage doesn't come because you are big, strong or without fear. Courage comes because you aren't big, you aren't strong, you do fear, but you don't give up!" ~*The Ellie Project*, Andrew Heard

Ask yourself this compelling question: *Who do I need to forgive?*

This may be an easy thing for you. Maybe it's, *I just need to forgive the other person for messing up our business transaction.* Or perhaps it's something more significant. Regardless of what you are dealing with, do not underestimate the power of forgiveness.

Forgiveness doesn't mean excusing the behavior. Often forgiveness has more meaning for you than for the person you are forgiving. Try looking at forgiveness as a gift. As corny as it sounds; forgiveness is the gift you give to yourself.

Bitterness and being unable to forgive are costly. Refusing to forgive someone else is like swallowing poison and hoping that they get sick. It's a cancer within a person. Martin Luther King Jr. said, "Let no man pull you low enough to hate him." It's true that the damage you do to yourself is way more detrimental than how your hate could ever affect others.

Unforgiveness will mess you up! I remember a man from years ago, who was a resentful, hateful man, and yet what was so sad was he was the one paying the biggest price. People had hurt him, yet his lack of forgiveness, his anger, and his bitterness was causing him physical pain. You could see it on his body as if it were as crumbling underneath the pain and the weight of resentment and anger.

Decide not to allow the actions of other people to take you out in the future. One of my mentors made this profound statement, "People are doing the best that they can. And all of my suffering is in the judgment of them." Let me say it again. "People are doing the best that they can. And all of my suffering is in the judgment of them."

As an example, imagine you are at a restaurant and ask for a glass of water, but the waitress never brings it. You get angry, and rant about the poor service, and your day is ruined. Meanwhile, this is your waitresses second job of the day, and so she has only had three hours of sleep. Her husband is in the hospital, and they have no insurance. And as you sat down, she just got a call from the school letting her know her daughter was in a fight, and she needs to come in. So, she is doing the best she can do, and yet you are suffering in judgment of her.

Now, it's nice to say people are doing the best they can until you're in that moment, right? When you're in the moment, you might be more apt to say, "I can't believe they did that to me." But maybe that person who just cut you off in traffic wasn't actually trying to ruin your day; they were just doing the best they could to get to the hospital. Maybe the person who forgot to return your phone call was coming down with the flu and barely functioning.

Here's an incredible distinction for you. Doing the best that you can doesn't necessarily mean you're doing what you know is right.

There's a difference between knowing right from wrong and doing the best you can. Sometimes we're doing the best we can even if it may not be the right thing to do.

Think about this extreme analogy: How could a person who came up to you on the street, held a gun to your head, and said, "Give me all your money," be doing the best they can?

Ask yourself, *What could be driving this man to take this action?* Maybe the man is in desperate need to feed his family, and this is the best strategy he knows to do that. He may be doing the best he can. Maybe his dire straits made him have a need to feel significant, and by holding a gun to your head, he feels like he has power. He is doing the best he can, but there is nothing right about it.

This statement gets really interesting when you apply it to your relationships.

As humans, there are several things we crave. As Tony Robbins states, humans have six major needs:

- The need for certainty and the need for variety.

- The need for significance and the need for connection.

- The need to grow and the need to give back.

Significance is a huge one. Do you think that if you went up to somebody, held a gun to their head and said, "Give me all your money." that you all of a sudden would feel significant? Absolutely. You ultimately become a very significant person in their life. So, maybe that man was struggling with either: *Should I take my life or should I do something else to gain significance?*

These six human needs drive most of our actions. And while you can step back and realize that people really are doing the best that they can, it doesn't mean that you need to allow them to hurt you. It doesn't mean that you will allow everyone to come into your life and do whatever they want. It doesn't mean you don't have boundaries. It means you are not going to judge them based on your stuff, your baggage, your current struggles.

Most often we see in others what we really don't want to see in ourselves. We might be critical of someone else for perpetually being late, but think we have good excuses for each time we are tardy. We might think our spouse doesn't give us enough attention, and completely ignore the fact that we stayed late at the office every day that week.

One day I was walking through the mall with a friend, and I noticed he had made several snide comments about some of the overweight people we passed. I finally turned and asked him how he was feeling about his own weight. Immediately he confessed how horrible he found his current weight, and that he really needed to do something about it. But it seemed to be easier to cast judgment on others than himself.

So, if you notice you are seeing all the angry people, it might be because you are wrestling with your own anger issues. Or maybe, you see a couple arguing in public, and you are quick to judge them, instead of feeling empathy. It might have something to do with your own relationship.

Being able to understand some of the reasons behind the actions of others offers us a huge benefit. The real opportunity comes in forgiving others and allowing yourself to move forward. The truth is, life becomes easier when you choose to accept the apology that you never got.

However, forgiveness is complex. As Debasish Mridha said, "To forgive others, you must forgive yourself first." The plot twist is that you need to not only forgive others, but you must have the ability to forgive yourself, too.

This is something that you have to work on, especially as a go-getter. Sometimes, it's easier to forgive other people than it is even to forgive yourself.

I want to walk you through this critical piece of your journey. Whether it's something small or huge, the real opportunity is in allowing yourself to forgive yourself. We can't move forward until we have released our grip of unforgiving to the past.

Even if I did something I knew I shouldn't have, I was doing the best of what I knew to do at that moment to get what I thought I needed.

We judge ourselves based on what we know now. We judge our past actions on what we know now.

Imagine that a little boy comes over to your home who's never seen a gas fireplace with those fake logs in the back, and the gas flames. The glass on those fireplaces gets incredibly hot. So, that little boy, who has never seen a gas fireplace before, thinks, *wow, that's beautiful.* Then he runs over and touches the glass.

Now, you may yell, "No, don't touch that! Be careful! Watch out!" You wouldn't walk over and scold, "You, stupid little boy, what is wrong with you? What are you thinking?"

You wouldn't judge him that way because he's never seen a fireplace like that before. He didn't know what he didn't know. That's how it is with ourselves.

Your mistakes or failures in the past, have often come from what you didn't know you didn't know.

There may be times in your life where you've touched that gas fireplace and said, "I will never do that again now that I know what it is." How silly would it be to yell at yourself, for doing something when you didn't know what it was? Just as foolish as it would be to yell at that little boy. Allow yourself to forgive yourself for not knowing in the past what you didn't know.

Let me say it this way: Forgiving yourself allows you to come back to the present.

Becoming aware of what's going on within you is powerful. If I'm depressed, usually it's because I'm living in the past. If I'm experiencing anxiety, usually it's because I'm living in the future, or I'm focused on what might happen in the future. If I'm at peace, usually that's because I'm living in the present.

Let's talk about what the path to forgiveness looks like.

First, acknowledge your anger and resentment. You might be angry at somebody else, or it might be at yourself. Find a way to say, "Here's why I am so pissed off." or "Here's why I'm so ticked off." It helps to actually physically write your reasons out. Acknowledge the pain, and acknowledge the hurt that you've received, and then realize: "This event hurt me because of this..."

I'm going to challenge you to write out your feelings. Don't just do this in your mind. There's a certain power that comes from writing out your emotions. As you write, you will go from the abstract to specific. If you don't want to write down the specific reason for your feelings, maybe you will want to write a letter that you'll never send instead.

Acknowledge, "Here's why this was painful. Here's why this made me angry. Here's how this hurt me. Here are the fears and self-doubt that this created within me."

You might want to ask yourself, *Is there any part of me that caused this situation?* Make sure you write it down. And then write down your answer to, *What was it that I was after that I didn't get, and what did that cause within me?*

The last piece is to choose to write your answers down and then let them go. Accept them for what they are. Learn the lesson, which we'll get to, and then let it go.

One of my favorite things about this topic of forgiving yourself is acknowledging that maybe now you're perfectly ready to take on the things that you failed at before. We talked earlier about making situations extreme, worse than they are and how some people may say, "I'm just terrible at relationships. I'll never get in a relationship again," and then throw in the towel. They beat themselves up, but the reality is because you failed in your first marriage, maybe you're perfectly ready for your next.

It has been said, "It is best to be the first child, the second spouse, and the third realtor." Before getting remarried, I told my now-wife, "The greatest thing about the fact that I was married before is I've learned a lot. I've learned all the things not to do, and we should be good to go."

Forgiveness is just as powerful in professional situations. Just because you messed up your first business doesn't mean you should never start another one. Give yourself credit for the things you learned from what went wrong the first time around. Now you are more prepared than ever to understand and handle the problems you are going to face.

It's how you perceive failure that makes such a big difference. As Eric Thomas said, "Failure is a bruise, it's not a tattoo."

Failure is something that we all experience, yet most of us are just trying to avoid pain the majority of our lives. At the same time, we are trying to avoid failure. The two actions often cancel each other out.

Most unsuccessful people are simultaneously trying to achieve success, while fighting hard to avoid failure. That is a recipe for a mediocre life. People who are living life right in the middle say, "I want to achieve success, and yet I want to avoid failure." As we know, any great success is going to involve failure along the way.

Recently I interviewed the incoming mayor of McKinney, Texas. I asked him, "Obviously you've experienced some failure. What have been some of your biggest missteps?" The reason I could say, "Obviously, you've experienced some failure," was not because of anything I had read in the news about him, but because in my eyes, he's a very successful man. He's accomplished some incredible goals. I've yet to meet a successful person who doesn't have a spectacular list of failures. To make my point, he laughed and agreed that he'd had many.

I've never met someone I've looked up to who didn't have an impressive list of all the ideas they'd tried that didn't work out. They've learned to accept that failure is part of the journey. If you're not succeeding fast enough, you're probably not experiencing enough failure. I sometimes ask my clients "How did you fail this week? Tell me one thing you did this week that didn't work out. Let's celebrate something you learned by something that didn't work out." All successful people know that success is a terrible teacher. You'll learn far more by failure than you ever will from success.

Remember, just because you failed doesn't mean you're a failure. This distinction was mind-altering in my own life.

Think about teaching a child to ride a bike. Right now, I'm teaching my son, Hudson, how to conquer that childhood rite of passage. When he rides his bike, and then when he falls off, I may say, "Oh, you fell. You're okay. Get back up." I don't walk over to him and yell, "You're a failure!" No, he just fell. He's not a failure. He simply fell.

It's interesting how we talk about kids learning, yet when we are adults learning something new, and we fall off, instead of saying, "Oh, we fell," we react and say, "I'm a failure." We make things so concrete when in reality it is a process. Look at yourself the way you look at small children. When they're learning to walk, you don't walk over go, "Dude, you've fallen down so many times. I think you should just give up." No, we encourage them: "You fell. Get back up. Get back up. Get back up."

We're so excited about kids trying new things when we're working with them. But then when we become adults, professional and mature, and somehow we begin to get uncomfortable with failure. I'm going to ask you to embrace failure and realize that it is part of the journey. It doesn't define you. It's an event, not a place you stay. You may have fallen, but you're not down for the count.

Falling down is how we grow. Staying down is how we die. I'm going to ask you to make the decision to feel the pain and move forward. Decide to allow yourself to have a failure but not call yourself a failure.

Let me give you some actions to take in accordance with this chapter.

First, I would love for you to have a Intentional Funeral. This is a writing exercise and transition process to evaluate the pain/failure, see it for what it was. The "funeral" enables you to acknowledge the facts, along with the feelings, and to then move forward. When you use this strategy to move through and feel the pain, it is quite powerful.

A prominent characteristic of this exercise is brevity. Make sure you don't have a five-year funeral. I remember when I used to call my coach and complain, and he would say, "All right, you have another 30 seconds to get it all out." It's okay to lay your failure and pain to rest. Just make sure the funeral has a quick and clear finish.

Write down your plan for your intentional funeral. If you've experienced pain or failure in the past, I want you to write it down to allow yourself to move forward. Go ahead and grab a piece of paper and title it: "The failure that I've experienced" or "The pain that I'm feeling now."

Acknowledge what is hurt. Then write down:

- What am I feeling?

- What would I have to believe to feel this way?

- What is the story I've created to feel this way? Am I the Victim or Victor?

- What is the lesson I can learn from this? And during this?

- What did I do great?

- What did I do wrong or poorly?

- What will I do better or different next time?

- What do I not have control of and cannot change?

- What is the next right decision?

Keep writing and acknowledge what goal you were after and what didn't work. For some of us, our strategy in going after an incredible goal might have been messed up. We don't need to give up on the goal. Sometimes we need to give up on the strategy. So, write down:

- What was I after, and what didn't work?

The last thing I want you to write down is that you've chosen to let it go. You made the choice to forgive yourself and move forward.

- I AM CHOOSING TO LET THIS GO.

This is a different process for everyone. How it goes for you depends on your pain, on who you are. There's no exact process for how to feel the pain and move forward. There isn't a 10-second recipe. Nobody else can tell you how you're going to process your pain. I think by understanding and walking through some of these models and strategies you can comprehend what's going on at a higher level. It will allow you to have more awareness and process your pain more effectively.

There's massive power in feeling the pain, acknowledging what the pain was, making the choice to forgive others, and then choosing to forgive yourself.

You're powerful, brave, and amazing, which is why you're reading this book. You know the potential you have within yourself. You know the love you have for others and the enthusiasm you have for the opportunities and accomplishments you're going to reach in your life. Do the work. Play it all in. Slow down in the present so that you can speed up later. Pay the price now, so you don't pay a more significant price down the road.

STEP 5

Ask the Right Questions

"Questions are the door to everything."
~W.S.

One of the most profound questions that I was ever asked was, "What is your purpose?"

For some reason, when the question was posed to me about five or six years ago, it resonated with me on a very high level. It caused me to pause and dig deeper within myself. If I'm not 100 percent clear on my purpose, then how am I making decisions?

What changed my life was when I got clear on that one question. When I got clear on my purpose, it allowed me to gain clarity in all areas of my life. I was able to place the different aspects of my life in alignment. By gaining clarity on my purpose, I was then able to make the right next decision because I knew ultimately where I wantcd to go.

My question for you is: What great questions are you asking?

Years ago, at a crossroads in my business, I asked myself, *Do I go all in on coaching and speaking, or do I focus more on practicing real estate?* What I realized was, I couldn't do both at a really high level. I had to make a choice. I began to ask myself specific questions, and they led me to realize that coaching, speaking and learning great strategies were the things that were most in alignment with who I chose to be.

My quest to discover my purpose started with great, strong questions. If you ask yourself wimpy questions, you're going to get wimpy answers. If you ask yourself great questions, you're going to get great answers.

Step Five: Ask Yourself Great Questions.

I'm going to ask you to dive in to step five. This is the moment. You've experienced failure on some level, or you've implemented a plan that hasn't worked out. Maybe you're experiencing pain. Let's turn a page.

This is your moment! Don't waste it. This is your opportunity to ask yourself great questions. To lean in and leverage the potential that's in this pain you might be suffering right now. You could ask yourself, *What can I learn in this moment?*

It has been said, "There are two kinds of real estate agents. There are people who have been in the business 20 years and have 20 years of experience. Then there are people who have been in the business for 20 years and have just one year of experience 20 times."

The people in the latter category don't learn anything. They don't ask better questions. Below, I'm going to give you some great questions to ask yourself as you're going through this process. These questions apply as you're going from the bottom to the top, as you're getting out of a relationship, as you're recovering, as you're taking the steps toward being a great you.

Here's what I want you to get out of this step: A lot of us are asking questions, but we're just not intentional about them. We ask questions of ourselves, but are your questions on autopilot, or are they sharp, intentional questions that are meaningful?

I'm going to give you some questions that I want you to answer. You can add these to your steps for getting back up. If you don't use mine, you can use your own. Write them down, make them powerful and personal.

When you find yourself in a hard spot, go down your list of questions and apply them to your situation. They will help you see the guidance in the experience. Don't waste the pain of the experience when instead you can learn the lesson.

Here is a good starter list of questions:

- What am I feeling?

- What would I have to believe to feel this way?

- What's the story that I am making up to feel this way?

- Will I be a Victim or a Victor?

- What is the lesson I can learn from this and during this?

- What did I do great?

- What did I do terrible or wrong?

- What will I do better and different next time?

- What do I not have control of and can't change?

- What do I have control of and can change?

- What is the next right decision?

You've probably heard people say ignorance is bliss. We know the reality is ignorance is bliss for a temporary moment, then it can be painful. Instead of choosing ignorance, ask the questions that could cause pain, especially when you're going through a tough period where you may experience a little bit of shame, hurt, anger, or guilt. But remember, the suffering is short term. Asking the questions now may cause short-term discomfort, but if we wait to ask them, it will cause a lot of long-term pain later on. Ignorance is not bliss.

Here is the first question I want to dive into: What can I control and what can I not control?

When you go through failure, or you have a negative event in your life, apply this question. You are fortunate to have the resources we discussed: time, energy and money. You get to control those resources even more when you ask this question and the other questions in this chapter.

You know these people who focus on what they can't control. Have you ever seen one of them go bowling? They step up to the line with the ball and just throw it down the lane. They wing it.

Then suddenly, as the ball begins to drift toward the gutter what do they do? They start to do a crazy dance, right? They spend a thousand times more effort *after* they throw the ball than they ever did getting ready. They spend all their energy and effort on something they can't control rather than spending the time, the energy and the effort on what they could have controlled: their stance, how they held the ball, how they released it.

We do the same thing in life. In the situation you are in, ask yourself: *What can I control? What can't I control?* Then make a choice. Successful people choose to spend their time, money, and energy on what they can control. They learn to release the things they can't control.

You can look at it as if it were a real estate agent who had a transaction fall apart. "This is horrible!" they say. They spend the next week freaking out about it and telling everyone the transaction fell apart as if their life is over. They're in the Storm the whole week complaining about it, whereas, the successful agent will say, "It is what it is." What they can't control is the fact this one deal fell apart. What they can control is what they do the rest of this week. They can analyze what went wrong and move on from there.

A slightly different version of that question is to ask yourself: *What can I not change and what can I change?* Determine the answer to those questions and then focus on what you can adjust.

There's a great equation for precisely this moment: **Situation X Response = Outcome** (The situation multiplied by your response equals the outcome).

There is a multitude of things that affect our lives from day to day, which we can choose to blame for not being where we want to be: the economy, our upbringing, a non-supportive spouse, lack of money, the weather, a new competitor... the list could go on and on. But the reality is, if we change our response to those situations, we can change our outcome.

Individuals who tend to blame everything and everybody before themselves believe an event happens and then there's no choice beyond an immediate response. Somebody cuts us off in traffic, and most people respond immediately. We start speaking in French. We suddenly know sign language.

In life, your response equals the outcome. Your response has an incredible impact on what your actual results will be. If instead of using French and sign language, what if you chose to let them drive on by? You could assume they were having an emergency, make sure you were out of their way, and go along with your day without all of the anger and agitation.

Most people think the events in their life are 90 percent of the outcome and that their response is just a small 10 percent. The longer I go into this journey, what I've realized is the event is only 10 percent. Your response is 90 percent of the actual results.

Event (10%) + Response (90%) = Outcome

How you're going to respond makes all the difference in the world. Underline that sentence! **How you're going to respond makes all the difference!**

Let's go back to the control segment. You can't always control the situation. You can't always control the environment. Sometimes, you can't control whether a business deal falls apart, or you lose a loved one, or someone walks out of a relationship. What you can control is your response. Your response will make all the difference.

Many people go through life being a victim of their situations. They want to blame the government. They want to blame taxes. They want to blame their parents. They want to blame anything and anyone else for the outcome. For their failures. For their limitations. Yet, the reality is that to achieve success, you must know it is your response that determines the outcome.

The other day, I was looking at a list of astounding rejection letters people have received. The thing that made them astonishing was that they all belonged to amazing people. Accomplished people like J.K. Rowling, the author of the Harry Potter series, were rejected over and over.

In 1956, Andy Warhol tried to donate a free piece of his artwork to the Museum of Modern Art and was asked to come pick it up, because they would not be able to use it. Today the Museum of Modern Art owns 168 pieces of Warhol's work.

I love Oprah; she's made such a significant impact in the world. She was fired from her first job because they said she was too emotional and nobody would ever remember her name. Some people would have said, "You know what? I guess that's true." They would have gone on not to live their dreams. Oprah's response made all the difference. She thought *I don't care what your opinion is. It can be yours. It doesn't have to be mine.*

All these amazing people were rejected by the experts, and it was their response that made all the difference. When I hit rock bottom, I had to make a choice of what my response was going to be.

Think about it this way, how many of us have gone golfing, and we've blamed the golf clubs for our failure. That's what it's like when you don't take control. Stop blaming. Start saying, "Here's what I can't control. Here's what I can control, and I'm going to choose a powerful outcome. I'm going to make the choice." The deciding factor for success is not going to hinge on external events. The deciding factor for success is going to be your response.

Tony Robbins talked about how people are either limited by their resources, or they become incredibly resourceful.

Unsuccessful people look at their resources and tell themselves, *This is all I have, it's not enough, I'm doomed.* They say, *I don't have enough money. That's why I can't do this. I don't have enough time. That's why I can't do what I'm supposed to do. I don't have enough people to support me. That's why I can't chase my dream.*

Successful people say, *I'm not going to be limited by my resources. I'm going to be somebody who's incredibly resourceful.*

This step reminds me of a story about Richard Branson. According to the Virgin Airlines website, several years ago he had gotten stuck in Puerto Rico while trying to get to the British Virgin Islands.

"They didn't have enough passengers to warrant the flight, so they canceled the flight," he explained.

I love this man. Sir Richard Branson doesn't think like anyone else. Here's how he thinks: *I'm going to see if I can find another way. I'm going to be resourceful.*

He continued his story, "I had a beautiful lady waiting for me in BVI, and I hired a plane and borrowed a blackboard and as a joke I wrote Virgin Airlines on the top of the blackboard, $39 one way to BVI. I went out around all the passengers who had been bumped, and I filled up my first plane." It didn't cost him a penny. They all paid their fee and he got to go see his girl.

The airline cancellation seemed insurmountable, but Richard Branson demonstrated that night one of the reasons he's been so successful. It's his resourcefulness. You've got to make a choice; are you going to be limited by your resources, or are you going to be an incredibly resourceful person?

One of your jobs, if you want to live up to your full potential, is responding quickly to changes. Look at a professional athlete. The team changes their formation. What do they need to do? They need to adjust fast. Your job is to respond that quickly to change.

There are two things you need to manage: you must control your thoughts, and you need to be aware of what you focus on. How you react and speak to yourself and others needs to represent your thoughts and your focus.

Your thoughts + What you focus on = Your experience

This equation directly relates to the questions that you ask yourself. You've got to manage your self-talk. New situations will cause new responses. New situations will also need for you to respond differently. Your response is going to make a dramatic impact on your experience as you walk out of your difficulties.

Years ago, a young married couple appeared on the show *Shark Tank*. They shared the heartbreaking story of their daughter passing away. I hope, and I pray that I never have to experience the loss of a child, I can't imagine that there's anything more painful.

Yet, as this couple went through that pain, when they were grieving their terrible event, they chose their response. They said, "What if we could do something in her name? What if we could honor our child, who we are never going to stop missing, who we're never going to stop being sad about, what if we could do something amazing and honor her?"

They went on to build an incredible company dedicated to funding orphanages in South Africa. Their response was, *We're going to honor our daughter. This is a terrible event, and still, we're going to do something good.* Their outcome is changing the lives of thousands and thousands of little kids. These children now have the opportunity to get medical attention, to go to school, and to benefit in countless ways because this couple chose to have their response benefit others.

You're going to have situations that show up in your life that are unfair. That you don't deserve. That you would pray that nobody must go through. But you get to make the choice on how you respond. You may do something spectacular with that pain.

An insightful question to ask yourself is: *Could there be a pattern in my life that I need to become aware of?*

Here is a follow-up that will be incredibly important for you: *What will you do differently next time?* This is where you work out how to move forward.

The reason I want you to write this down is because of the philosophy I have adopted: **As we grow our business, we write every wrong.** What that means is every time something doesn't work out, I write down what I'm going to do differently next time, or what step I missed in the process. I don't just ignore it. I don't pretend it's not going to happen again. I write down the steps of what I'm going to do differently moving forward.

Write every wrong. Write what you did well, what you did poorly, and the lesson you've learned so you know what to do differently moving forward. As you're asking yourself these questions, one of the things you may begin to become aware of is an inner critic in your head beating you up. This voice reminds you of all the things you're not doing well and the mistakes you've made.

The Inner Critic

Something I read about years ago in the brilliant book, *Success Principles* by Jack Canfield, was the process of transforming your inner critic. This process focuses on teaching your inner critic to tell you the whole truth, not just the negative. Criticism lives in the realm of fear and anger, but that only tells you part of the truth.

The whole truth is that the message has four phases:

- Anger – *I'm mad at you...*
- Fear – *I'm afraid of what could happen to you...*

- Requests – *I want you to be smarter/safer...*
- Love – *I love you. I want you safe, happy, and healthy...*

Canfield explains how, when we were kids, our parents told us not to run into the street, or to stay off the counter, or to leave the ladder alone. We listened to the first part of what they were saying, but we didn't hear the rest. The first part of what they were saying is to stop; don't do that. But what they were saying underneath was, *I love you. Be careful. I love you. Don't get on the counter, because you could fall.*

Because of our inner critic, we often just hear the first part with anger. Your inner critic is saying; *You're lazy. If you were a better person, you would get up earlier in the morning.* But underneath that anger, is phase two.

Phase two is fear. Underneath all the talk of, *You're an idiot for not getting up in the morning. What's wrong with you? Why aren't you getting up?*, is a fear. That is your subconscious mind actually saying, *I'm fearful if I don't get up earlier in the morning. For one, my body's not going to be as healthy as it needs to be. And two, I'm not going to have the success that I know I can have.*

Underneath fear is a request for who you really are. The request is, *I would love for you to get up earlier in the morning and be able to go to the gym. Be able to start your workday better so that we can have the life we want to have.* At the foundation is, *I really love you. I care about you. I want you to have a great life.*

Transform the inner critic. Take it from, *You're an idiot for not getting out of bed earlier,* to *What's really going on? What am I afraid of? I want to have a big life.*

Underneath the fear is, *What's the real request?* When I beat myself up, I know it's probably because there's a real authentic request buried under the anger and fear. Underneath that request is actually love.

If you can transform your critic from not just hearing the anger, but to going deep through those four phases and discovering the love and the true intention, it will begin to transform your life.

Questions Are Incredibly Powerful

Next, there are several more questions I am going to give you. Yes, I'm giving you a lot of questions but remember, questions are incredibly powerful. My coaching clients often call me a "question geek."

If you're looking to learn both the answer and the lesson, here are some revealing questions you can ask yourself:

- What would someone I respect or someone I admire do in this situation?

- What's the lesson they would learn?

I love watching some of the interviews with Elon Musk. He's done insane things with electric cars and rockets and everything else.

One time, his rocket was supposed to come down and land on a platform. Well, the rocket came down, touched the platform, and then the whole thing tilted over and blew up. I love that Elon didn't sit back and say, "Oh my goodness! I can't believe that happened. We wasted all this money." Nope. He figured he had learned one approach that was not going to work. Then he immediately transferred his thoughts to a new game plan.

Often, I'll ask myself, how do I think Elon Musk would respond to the situation?

How would Sir Richard Branson respond to this situation?

What's the lesson they would learn, and would they move on?

Would they keep going? Of course, they would.

Ask yourself:

- What's the one thing I can learn from this?
- What is something I can alter?
- How can I adjust my trajectory moving forward to avoid this situation next time?
- Was there something about my strategy that was not effective?
- Do I need to change that?
- What's the one thing that I will do differently next time?

Make sure you write your answers down.

Many of us have experienced failure. You might even be going through these steps right now. You might ask yourself some of these questions. What is so brilliant about this process, and why the nine steps are so powerful, is your ability to answer those questions.

Go through this in a systematic, intentional way where the process is not an abstract or generality in your mind. Walk through these steps purposefully, and you will learn that is where the answer is. That's what allows you to move faster. Having a process and a system in place *before* you need it is what's going to be such a radical advantage in your life. Doing this will separate you from so many others.

I Am

Let me give you one more lesson I learned before we move on. I discovered a very hardcore insight when I was at my lowest. I hope you're ready to read it.

My self-identity was shaken at rock bottom. I discovered I had placed my identity in what I did, in being a successful real estate agent, in being a successful businessman, in being a great man, a great husband, being involved in the church, I had placed my identity in what I did, not who I was.

I'm going to challenge you with an exercise that is seemingly simple, yet profound. This is what I did, and I want you to do it, too. Write down simple "I am" statements. For example, I wrote down, "I am smart." "I am capable." "I am resourceful." "I am loving." "I am kind." "I am full of energy."

Here's what's thought-provoking: Have you ever written or thought an "I am" statement like "I am wealthy," and suddenly your inner critic responds with *Oh, you are? Really? Go look at the bank account.* All of a sudden, your mind says, *That's BS; that's ridiculous.* I'll say, "I'm a great dad," but a little part in my mind will shoot back, *Really? Because I think you dropped the ball.*

Here's how you get around that mental roadblock, you change how you ask yourself these powerful questions. If I am battling my inner critic, I would ask myself, *What about me makes me a great dad? I'm a great dad because I'm doing my best. I'm a great dad because I put my child's needs before my own.*

If I would say, I am wealthy, that flips to, *What about me makes me wealthy?* That is a mind hack to get you to believe yourself. Automatically I'm forcing my subconscious mind to find some positive answers.

Here's a recap of step five: Write down the questions you're going to ask yourself. Plan how to move through the inner critic to get from anger to love. Then I would implore you to do this, write down just five "I Am" statements so you can begin to identify who you are, not what you do.

Some of my personal "I Am" Statements

- I AM love

- I AM empowering

- I AM smart

- I AM capable

- I AM resourceful

- I AM fully present

- I AM worthy of receiving the best in life

- I AM wealthy

- I AM creative

- I AM lovable

- I AM healthy

- I AM persistent

- I AM determined to succeed

- I AM blessed every day

- I AM grateful for all of the people in my life

- I AM able to help others

I know that if you're reading this book, you are someone who has boundless potential. You're someone who doesn't settle. You're someone who believes you have greatness within you. The cool thing is if you see any greatness within somebody else, or greatness within me, it means you have it within yourself.

Do the work. Write this stuff out. See you in Step Six.

STEP 6

Make the Next Right Decision

*"Our main business is not to see what lies dimly at a distance,
but to do what lies clearly at hand."*
~Thomas Carlyle

Years ago, I was able to have breakfast with David Norberg, a top producing realtor since 1989 in San Diego County. I love this man. He is brilliant, soft-spoken and has a huge heart. As we were sitting and talking, I asked him, "What were some of the defining moments in your life? What are some of the things that made the biggest difference? If I were your son, what advice would you give to me? "

He told me about how, early on in his life, he had gone through some rough patches. At one point, he was literally homeless, sleeping in his car. It was freezing outside, and he realized, "Holy cow, I'm sleeping in my car. I am homeless." In his perception, he had hit rock bottom.

I asked, "Well, what did you do to get out of there? What was the one thing that made all the difference?"

He said, "I began to make decisions. I realized that making decisions was incredibly hard for me, and I really struggled with making some of the big decisions."

He went on, "I started with making little ones. I had a decision muscle that I needed to start working." So, if someone said, "Do you want to go here, or do you want to go there?" he would just make a decision. If he went to order a sandwich, he would make a decision on what he wanted. He started with small decisions and worked that decision muscle until he could make more significant decisions with a sense of certainty.

Step Six: Make the Next Right Decision

Most of us struggle with decisions. We struggle with decisions when we're in a great place, let alone when we're in the whirlwind or the Storm of difficulty. When we're in the Storm of *I've just gone through a failure*, or *I'm struggling*, it's hard.

Norberg's lesson is so powerful and teaches us the next thing we need to do after learning the lessons. After you've felt the pain, you've got to make the next decision. What are you going to do to get back up? The reality is there are many options.

I see people in the business world struggling all the time. They will question, "What should I do?" And it's because they have so many options in front of them. The more options you have, the harder it is to make a decision. The most powerful thing you can do when you're in the Storm is to make the next decision.

One of the most profound things that I learned from a coach was the understanding that there's not always a right decision. I grew up believing there was always a wrong decision and a right decision. There were never two right decisions. What my coach helped me realize was that sometimes in life there are just decisions and it's my job to make them right. Along these same lines, I once heard a speaker say, "There is not always one right decision. I always want to make the right decision, yet I will put way more energy and effort into making that decision right than getting stuck by not making the decision at all."

I want to give you some of the tactics you can use to help you make impactful decisions, but understand, you still have to make a decision. It was Steve Jobs who said, "One of the things that's tough about this life is it's difficult to connect the dots looking forward. You can only connect the dots looking back."

Many times, you simply have to make the decision, then go make it right. If it wasn't the best decision, you have the ability to change it. But you've got to freaking make a decision. I would rather work with someone who will make a decision, and then if it's wrong, correct it, than someone who would get so rattled they can't make a choice at all.

In hard times, we often get stuck. Do I turn left, or right? Do I go forward, or turn back?

One of my friends said, "One of the greatest things I've done to become a success was that I wasn't afraid to make decisions. I realized I was a resourceful, whole person, and if I made the wrong decision, I would correct it. I had to make decisions."

Let me give you some effective tactics you can use in this decision-making process. Years ago, I was introduced to the

G.R.O.W. Model which was developed by Graham Alexander and racing champion, Sir John Whitmore. What I love about this model it is simple.

G.R.O.W. is an acronym for Goal, Reality, Options, and Way.

G is for Goal.

First, you need to ask yourself: What is my goal?

For simplicity's sake, let's assume I'm using this in the context of working with a real estate agent.

Me: "What was your goal for contacts?"

Agent: "My goal was to make 80 great contacts."

R is for Reality.

Me: "Awesome, what was the reality?"

Agent: "The reality was I made 40."

Me: "Okay so your goal was 80; you made 40."

O is for Options.

Me: "First off, great job on getting 40. Let's brainstorm. For you to hit 80 next week, what are some of your options? What are some ways we can get to 80 next week? Let's just spitball these, throw them up against the wall."

Agent: "Well, I could call the people who live around my new listing, I could go door knocking before my open house, call the rest of my database, call past clients..."

Me: "Perfect! Those are wonderful."

W is for Way.

Me: "Now, what's the way? Which one of these five or six options are you going to choose to accomplish your goal next week?"

The Grow Model will focus your thoughts and give you actions to choose from to reach your goals. What's your goal? What's the reality? What are the options? Then which one do you chose to help you get there? This is one of several great tactics you can use, many of which I teach weekly in The Hero Nation FUEL.

G.R.O.W. is just one of several tactics we will be covering in this chapter. You can explore these tactics and choose which ones you want to use in the future. Write down the strategies which feel like the best fit for you and your situation.

One basic starting strategy is to discover what you're ultimately after. In other words, what is the end you desire to achieve?

You have to get clear on what you're after. You can say, "I want to get back to my feet." Well, what does that specifically look like? How will you know when you are "back on your feet"? Why do you want that? Figuring out what you're really after is an essential piece of this process.

An additional strategy is to write down some of your fears, so you at least know what you're up against. Then, you can determine if those concerns are legitimate and how likely they are to be an issue. Once you discover that, you can take steps to avoid those fears from manifesting

Stepping back and pretending you're advising a friend is another step you can take, and one that I love. I use this all the time with my clients. I'll say, "What do you think you should do next?" When they reply, "I don't know." I'll ask them "OK. If you were coaching or giving counsel to someone in your exact same position, what would you tell them to do?" This is an effective way to pull yourself out of your normal view so that you can see the reality from another perspective. Asking that question can feel weird, but it triggers a different part of the brain. Because of that new stimulus, you will come up with some previously undiscovered brilliance.

Another strategy would be to call a friend, a mentor, or your coach. Be smart about who you call. Call someone you trust, someone who is going to give you great advice. There are lots of people you can call up and tell them, " I'm stuck." And they might just say, "Aw, that sucks. I'm so sorry." They will just join you in the mud puddle.

If you're going to call a friend, you need to call someone who's not going to buy into your story. Meaning, they're not going to allow you to compile all the excuses why you can't. This should be a person who's going to help you cut through what's troubling you and give you sound advice.

My friend, Hank Avink had a good warning for this scenario, "Never take advice from someone you wouldn't trade places with."

One method I mentioned earlier was to ask yourself, *What would someone I look up to do in this situation?* As I said in step five, sometimes I'll ask myself, *What would Richard Branson do with this puzzle? What would my father do in this situation? How would some of the people who give me advice approach this scenario?*

With these questions you can also use the time-traveler trick. Envision it is twenty years from now, and then get curious. *In twenty years from now, what would do? What would my advice be for me right now?*

These are some of the ways to trigger the resourcefulness you have within you. Use them as strategies to ignite the wisdom inside you. You have far more brilliance in you than you probably know. You must tell yourself you are a capable and talented person and then activate your excellence.

For some of you who are very detailed and prefer to see it all laid out, a spreadsheet may work very well for you. Write out all your different options. Like mom used to tell us, make lists of the pros and the cons for each choice. Don't forget to ask yourself how each of the options affect not only yourself but how do they affect the people around you. What's the expected outcome of each one?

If you're not gelling with the spreadsheet idea, you can also go with your gut. Trust who you really are. Now, if you're in the midst of the Storm, you're going to struggle with making a decision. At the same time, you might often know in your heart what the next right option is. You may have to come to terms with it. You may have to wrestle with it a bit, but you probably know on some level what the choice is that you need to make.

A tactic that is very powerful for me is to reflect on past wins. You can ask yourself: *When was a time in the past that I wrestled with a problem like this, a time that I made a decision, and it worked out?* Go back and identify what worked in the past, that may work in the future. Grab some of that energy from the past and pull it into the present.

Tony Robbins calls this "Getting Certain." And when you do this, you gain confidence and certainty in knowing, *I have survived times like this in my past and because of that, I know I can get through it again.*

The last four tactics I am about to share with you are vitally important. Make sure you always include them in your future planning.

First: Self-reflect. Look at yourself and the options you've laid out, then ask yourself these questions: *Do they line up with my values? Do they line up with my core beliefs? Are they in alignment with who I am and where I'm going?*

Don't make a decision that would violate your core values even if it's what you think may move you forward. Make sure whichever choice you make is in alignment with who you are and where you're going.

What do you value? What's important to you? Don't get it twisted. Don't do something that conflicts with who you are or that's in conflict with where you're going. An extreme example would be robbing a bank to feed your family when your core belief is to keep integrity in all things. When it comes to core values, seldom does the end justify the means.

Second: Release the belief that there's a perfect decision. Let go of the idea that there's one magic decision out there that's going to make it all better. I promise you, most of the time, almost all the time, there's not one perfect mystical decision. Too often we look for that magic pill, that answer that's going to make all the difference. Very rarely does it exist. It's easy to connect everything looking back; it's hard to connect the dots looking forward. Usually, you just have to make a choice.

Third: Stop thinking about what you are going to do and make a decision. At some point, you've got to choose what to do. I'm not saying it's easy, yet you've got to make a decision.

We discussed earlier the question, "Do you make decisions or do you self-sabotage until they are made for you?"

Don't wait until you are painted into a corner. Give yourself a time limit; by this time, I am going to make a decision. Then stick to it.

Fourth: Once you make that decision take the massive action and I mean MASSIVE action!

There is a compelling quote by Edward Teller that drives home the meaning of this chapter: "When you come to the end of all the light you know, and it's time to step into the darkness of the unknown..." He said one of two things are probably going to happen. Either you're going to find there's something there for you to step on or you're going to discover how to build some wings as you fall.

The reality is you've got to make a decision and allow yourself to know that you can recover and that you can adjust down the road if you need to. You've got to make the decision and release the belief that there's a perfect decision.

Go through this process to help you identify your best decision and then make it.

You might say, "I'm going to do this one thing to move me forward."

Maybe your transactions all fell apart. You can say, "I'm in the Storm. What's the one thing I've got to do? The one thing I've got to do is start contacting new people."

Whatever it is, take massive action. Don't wimp out. Don't tell yourself that your action is to contact two people. No, you need to take giant leaps. If you're in the process of getting out of the pit, getting back up, you've got to make monumental movement. If you need to make contacts, make 40, 50, 60 contacts the next day. The most successful people will make a decision and then they'll take significant steps on one or two things. They don't worry about everything else.

Decide to focus on those one or two things and go all in. Don't settle. Don't play easy. Go all in.

Figure out and then write down what your process is going to be when you struggle with a decision in the future. As you write your process down, realize that there may or may not be a perfect decision. You're going to make the best decision that you know is in alignment with the people that you care about and your core values.

Make a decision and take massive, *massive*, MASSIVE action because that's what you have within you. Taking MASSIVE action will get you out of your tough spot faster and more effectively than anything else.

One of the most powerful things that people who struggle with low self-esteem can do to change the way they view themselves is to take action. You don't just find self-worth and put it on like a shirt. I don't care how many little cute quotes you read on Facebook; those are not going to help you. The way to feel better about yourself is by doing the things you're afraid of doing, by taking action when you don't know how to take action.

You go and get self-esteem. You earn self-esteem. Self-esteem is generated from the inside. Nobody else can give it to you. You create it by doing what you are afraid of doing, by doing the hard stuff. What are people the proudest of at the end of their life? They are proudest of the challenges they got through, of the action they were afraid of taking but took anyway. When you take massive action, at the end of the day, you can be proud of the person you are.

I love you, my friends. I will see you in Step Seven.

STEP 7

You're Not Alone

"What is most personal is most universal."
~Carl R. Rogers, On Becoming a Person: A
Therapist's View of Psychotherapy

A little while ago I was in San Diego at a remarkable retreat with some incredible high-achieving men. The first night we sat down around an outdoor fireplace and talked about life, work, and how to grow our empires to a whole new level. Then we chatted about some of the roadblocks in our businesses, some of the areas where we were stuck.

One of the men opened up and shared that he had recently struggled with depression, and even with thoughts of suicide. It was tough for him to share because of the judgment he expected to get. Keep in mind; this is a group of men that from outside appearances are succeeding at every level. I mean, these are absolutely stellar dudes.

I asked the group, "How many of you have struggled with depression within the past couple of weeks, or months?" Every single one of those men raised their hand. Every single one of them acknowledged they had fought with depression, or with not being able to get back up, or with being in that "stuck" place. And here's what was so interesting about that moment: What's most personal is most universal. Often we think that we're the only one struggling; that there's something wrong with us because we're dealing with depression. Or we feel that something is wrong with us because we don't know how to get up and we don't feel like we're enough. Well, welcome to the freaking crew, right?

The reality is, we all struggle with this sort of stuff from time to time. Now, that's not an excuse to wallow in the puddle; I just think it's helpful to acknowledge you're not alone.

Step Seven is: Acknowledge, realize, and accept the fact that you are not alone.

As you go through your obstacles, don't forget that other people are struggling, too. What I've discovered in the last several years from working with thousands of people all over this country is, almost every single person has something they're battling that nobody else knows about. With nearly every single person I've encountered, who I went to a deep level with, I've discovered they had something intense going on. Either they were deeply worried about money, or they had a relationship they were trying to hold together, or they were about to suffer a loss. Whatever it was, everybody has something they're fighting. Usually, most other people are unaware of these individual struggles going on around them.

You're not alone. One of the most impactful steps you can take is to acknowledge this fact and then gather with a group of people who will support you.

The first action I want you to take is to recognize this reality. It is such an easy step, and it sounds like I am just repeating myself, but you need to simply recognize that you're not alone. Accept that other people have been through these hard times as well and that they have made it past the experience. So, you can, too.

Many famous people have struggled with depression. As a spectator, you would never guess, but people like Jim Carrey, Johnny Depp, and Eminem have all battled it. Even Harrison Ford and Angelina Jolie have openly talked about their depression.

Michael Phelps revealing his struggles with depression is something I will always a remember. His confession was surprising when reflected against the extraordinary accomplishments of this uniquely high-achiever. In an interview a couple of years ago, he talked about how, starting after his second Olympics, he struggled with depression. He continued to experience that pattern after each subsequent Olympics.

The build-up and intensity of the event lead to a mental crash once his focus was gone. He began a cycle of substance abuse, to escape "whatever it was I wanted to run from." Just weeks after winning eight gold medals at the Beijing Olympics, a picture circulated of him using a bong. He said he began to battle with depression at an incredibly deep level, to the point where he didn't even know why he was here anymore.

A couple of years later, after struggling for a long time, he checked himself into rehab to wholly and finally recover. From the outside looking in, we question, "Are you kidding? That guy is truly amazing, look at all his medals; look at everything he has accomplished!" But his reality was that some circumstances in his life weren't working. His beliefs conflicted with each other, and he was struggling at a very high level.

It's easy for us to look at other people and think, *They've got it all together. I'm the only one having difficulties.* I think especially in this day and age, and due in part to platforms like Facebook, you'd swear all your friends are on vacation all the time; they all have perfect marriages; everything is just ideal all the time. We judge what's going on in us, in our real world, against what we perceive is happening in the worlds of others. Doing this can cause us to spiral downward.

Once you have acknowledged that you aren't alone in your struggles, I'm going to give you some tactics to help you when you are in a tough place. These tactics not only apply to you, but they enable you to help others in a tough spot as well.

How do you help people when they're struggling? One of the best ways to help people is by asking them the right questions. The question that I want to focus on now is: "How do you find good friends?"

Well, the first way you find good friends is by being a great friend. I'm going to teach you some ways you can help other people when they're struggling, whether it is depression or they're trying to get up out of a hole. It won't matter if they fell in the hole or whether they dug it and jumped in.

As kids, how did we find our friends? We found the people that lived on the block, or who went to school with us. That worked out well while we were younger. The problem is, we begin to carry that same child-like strategy into adult life. As we become adults, who are our friends? Usually, the people that live on the block, or they're the people we work with or the people we're in some involvement with to some degree. Yet, that's probably not the best way to find the significant people you need to have in your life. Great people may not live next door. They may not be the people that are in the office with you. You've got to go find the right people.

Years ago I had the realization that I needed some new friends. I needed to level up some of my friendships. It sounds kind of weird, but I sat down and wrote out the description of who the people would be that I would love to have in my life. I asked myself, *Who were some of the friends that I would choose to have?* I wrote down that they would probably be married like me. They probably had kids. I wanted them to have similar values to mine. I wrote down the criteria of who those people were, knowing those new friends wouldn't just appear unless I was actively seeking them out.

Most great friendships aren't just going to appear; you've got to get clear on what you desire, and what you're looking for, and then go after them.

One of my best friends is Hank Avink. We've had to foster our relationship. We've spent time on the phone. We've had times where we didn't agree and then we worked through it. We've had times where we didn't talk for a while, and then we were purposeful and began to talk again.

You've got to find those friendships and pour into them. Now what I love is that I've got some great people in my life. I've got people in my life that know if I'm in a tough place I need one of three things: a hug, a hand up, or a kick in the butt.

Surround yourself with the right people. The right people will know what you need. They won't bind your story. They will help you through the rockier phases of your life.

You're going to be a great friend, so I'm going to give you some specific strategies you can use when someone else is struggling. Here's what's terrific about true friends: true friends aren't the ones that make your problems disappear. They're the ones who don't disappear when you have problems. They're the ones who show up.

Here are some of the ways you can show up for those people that you love, that you care about, and that you want to help. The first thing to do is just make contact. Be there. Show up for them and listen. Often, especially for high achievers, we don't always need somebody to tell us what to do. The need is more about having somebody there to talk things out with. For me, it is having someone to listen to my story for a minute, to call me on my BS, and yet be present with me.

True friends won't make a problem or situation seem like the end of the world, and they won't pretend like it's nothing either. They're the ones who will be there during the pain but also acknowledge that I'm the one who's got to do the work.

Great friends won't push. They'll help you make decisions. They'll give you advice. They won't tell you what you need to do.

They'll guide you. They're not going to shove you into doing something. They're going to help you discover and maybe ask some thought-provoking questions. If someone is going through tough times, the most crucial things I believe you can do is be present, listen, ask them questions. This is how you help them to become resourceful. Help them to dig within themselves to find the answers, to find what they needed to do next, to move through their ordeal.

Another way to be a great friend is to realize that emotions will come in waves. Some days, especially depending on the struggle, there will be highs and there will be lows. Be present with your friend. Don't expect them to be all better in an instant. Don't assume that because they felt great one day that it's going to be that way from now on. Be there but allow them to have their own process.

The nine steps in this book make an excellent framework for how to go from rock bottom to getting back up. They're a roadmap for you to use when you need it most. But remember, everyone goes through their process differently. Allow the people in your life to move through their rough patches on their own terms, to process their journey in the way that they need to.

As they are working through their challenges, another thing you can do is be aware of their triggers. For example, if someone is recovering from alcohol, you may not want to meet them at the bar. If you know someone recently lost their pet, you probably don't want to constantly talk about your dog. Rally support and realize that at some point you may go through tough times, too. Model what you think is best; be a role model of how you would like them to treat you.

Finally, be encouraging. Encourage and support your friends in some of their smaller wins. Understand that nighttime and the end of the day are usually the toughest. Remind them that tomorrow may be better. Be there with them; support them; be patient on their journey.

Also, you may need to help them avoid reckless behavior. Sometimes when you're going through something tough you'll want to go spend all your money or give into other impulses to make the pain go away. If your friend is feeling like that is a way to help them numb the pain, be there for them, help them, make sure they stay within reasonable limits.

At the end of the day recognize this: I believe that most of us have a sincere desire within ourselves to be accepted. We want to be more than just being accepted on the surface; most people crave one person in the world to accept them for who they are, for all their stuff, drama, mistakes, screw-ups, and all their greatness. That's what we're after. Most of us just want to someone who comes beside us and says, "You know what? I love you, the uniquely wonderful, mess, disaster, amazing, great, awesome, horrible, (whatever) person you are. I love you for who you are." If you can be that person to someone else, that's freaking incredible. I don't know if there's a greater gift that you can give someone, than accepting where they are, and at the same time seeing their greatness of where they can go.

If you want to get through tough times, go out and realize you're not the only one. Build a group of friends who will support you at a high level and yet won't let you off the hook. They'll call you on your stuff, but still support you when you need it. Build that group of friends. Then become a great friend to others. Be someone who accepts other people for where they're at, who realizes everybody has their own struggles.

Everybody is going through their own stuff. It doesn't mean you let them off the hook if they're going to make a bad decision. It means that you support them and love them in the right way.

This is one of the main reasons I started The Hero Nation Mastermind, a community of amazing high achievers who don't apologize for being awesome and are real about our struggles.

To wrap up step seven, this is where you acknowledge that you're not alone. Pre-plan for rough times. Be intentional about the people that you let into your world. Be intentional about the friends that you have. If you want to have great friends in tough times, be a great friend when your friends are going through tough times.

Most people have a deep desire when they're in a tough time for someone to be there for them. They want that strong person who will come into their world and accept them: the good, bad, and the ugly. I've gone through hard stuff, and I was not the person I would want to hang out with. Yet, I had great friends who would come into my world and be with me, who would accept me for the crazy, amazing, screwed up, awesome, terrible, wonderful, confused, loving, kind person I was.

If you want to get through difficult times, be a friend to others during difficult times, and prepare to have great and invaluable people in your life when it is your turn to experience the roller coaster.

I'll see you in Step Eight.

STEP 8

Build Your First-Aid Kit (Pouring in the Good Stuff)

"Spectacular achievement is always preceded by unspectacular preparation."
~Robert H. Schuller

A young boy is sitting on the front porch of a farmhouse next to his grandfather. The boy looks up at his grandfather and says, "Grandfather, sometimes I feel sad but there's another side of me that fights to feel happy. What do I do?"

The grandfather looked down and said, "Let me tell you a story about two wolves. In all of us, there are two wolves. One wolf is angry, full of resentment, sadness, despair, and depression, and another one is full of happiness and joy and love and kindness and compassion. They're at battle with each other."

The little boy looked up at his grandfather and asks, "Well, Grandpa, which one of them wins?"

The grandfather looked down with the wisdom of decades in his gaze and said to his young grandson, "The one that you feed will win the battle."

Step Eight is Building Your First-Aid Kit and Proactively Preparing for Tough Times.

The art of getting back up is about you making the conscious decision to pour in the good stuff.

When you have rough times, or you hit rock bottom and you're working to get back up, it is critical to make sure you aren't filling your mind with negativity. You may not be able to handle things as you did when you were in peak state. It might be a better choice to not to listen to the news every morning, to avoid hearing about all the terrible things that are happening in the world. You might want to avoid the water cooler gossip or refrain from calling your mother-in-law. Whatever your decision, I want you to free up opportunities to pour in the good stuff.

Think of it this way; you don't buy a first-aid kit after you cut your finger. You buy a first-aid kit and you put it in your home, way before you need it, so it's ready. That's what I want you to do. I want you to pre-plan for rough times. In other words, if I hit a rough patch, if I'm struggling with anger or depression, frustrated or wondering how the heck I will get back up, I have a first- aid kit. I have a pre-planned list of things I'm going to do to get back up, to get my emotional state and my head in the right place.

There are five different areas that you need to pre-plan for:

1. My mindset

2. My business

3. My relationships

4. My body

5. My time

How am I going to pre-plan for rough times? What am I going to do to take care of those five critical areas of my life? Let's dive into each one of these categories.

Let's start with your mindset. Isn't that where it all starts anyway? As it relates to your mind, there are several things I want you to do. The first is to refer back to your "I am" statements in Step Five: *I am resourceful. I am smart. I am capable*, etc. Have those statements ready to go to remind yourself who you really are. Then become aware of the conversations in your mind. Choose awareness, choose to go from beating yourself up to loving yourself. Have a plan that you can use to accomplish this. We've already talked about the four questions you can ask yourself to get through that process.

Another way you can take care of your mind is to ask yourself how you are processing each week. One of the things that I love and that I teach my clients is to wrap up the week in an impactful way. Ask yourself the questions that demonstrate you're taking care of your mind throughout the week. *What worked this week and what didn't work?* Reflect upon the week, and ask yourself, based on the results of this week, *Is there anything that I should stop doing? Is there anything that I should start doing?* Ask yourself, *Where's my focus?*

Where your focus goes, your energy flows. So, where are you focusing?

Full list of WEEKLY QUESTIONS TO ASK YOURSELF and more at www.TheArtofGettingBackUp.com.

One of the most transformative things you can do, especially in a state of turmoil, is to force yourself to meditate. It may sound funny, but I often have to force myself to take a moment and meditate for 10 minutes.

I remember years ago when one of my coaches told me to start meditating I asked, "What do you want me to do? What do you want me to think about? What do you want me to listen to?" I kept asking him all these questions and he said, "Wayne, I just want you to shut up for 10 minutes and not do anything."

Meditation is one of the things I've begun to force myself to do, and I say force because it wasn't easy for me. If I get anxious or if I'm feeling worried or depressed, I stop, take a break, just lie on the floor and meditate for 10 minutes. For me, this usually means I simply shut up. I don't think about it; I merely take a moment for peace.

In this world of chaos where our phones are dinging and our music is playing we've always got something going on. It's eye-opening how rejuvenating a couple of moments of silence can be. Take care of your mental wellbeing by allowing your conscious mind to have moments where nothing's going on.

Another question you can ask yourself is: What can I do to clean up some space in my mind? What can I declutter? What are some of the things in my mind I can get rid of?

Many of us have excessive amounts of stuff floating around in our brains, and it causes a lack of clarity and anxiety in our lives.

We have too much stimulus in our world and a massive degree of information coming at us at all times that we try to retain. I see this condition in the eyes of my clients frequently. I call it Self-Induced-Overwhelm, which when unattended will lead to a crash and burn scenario.

Often, I tell my clients to do a mind-dump. A mind-dump is when you sit down with a blank piece of paper and write out all the things in your mind. Write everything from change the oil and send your mother a birthday card, to check on this and pay that. Whatever it is take half an hour and get all that stuff out of your mind and onto a piece of paper. Free up some mental space.

Your mind is like a computer. If you've got way too many windows open, your computer will shut down. If you've got too many things on your mind, it'll cause you to get stuck. Use some strategies to get that content out of your mind and onto paper so you can process it.

In this first-aid kit in your mind create a list of the books you're going to read. Some of my all-time favorites are *Who Moved My Cheese?* by Spencer Johnson; *How to Stop Worrying and Start Living*, Dale Carnegie; 7 *Strategies for Wealth & Happiness* by Jim Rohn; *Think and Grow Rich*, Napoleon Hill; and *You Are a Badass? How to Stop*

Doubting Your Greatness and Start Living an Awesome Life by Jen Sincero.

Make an effort to read scriptures or quotes that reinforce your purpose, re-inspire, and keep you focused. I have different quotes on the wall around me in my office and they often remind me to get back to center; they tell me to focus on the most important things in my life.

Another thing I'm going to ask you to do to take care of your mind is to begin to track your wins. I use a journal called the Best Self Journal. Every morning the journal asks me to do two things: Write down what I'm grateful for and write down some of my wins from the last couple of days.

Gratitude and fear can't live in the same place, so I am also intentional about what am I going to read, and the questions I'm going to ask myself. For instance, *What am I NOT going to allow in my world? What are the quotes I'm going to dive into? What are the books I'm going to read?* Track your wins and give gratitude.

This next area is pre-planning for your first-aid kit as it applies to taking care of your business. Unfortunately, when tough times arise most of us don't have the luxury of not tending to our business. We don't have the luxury of taking three months off. You've got to run your business while you're taking care of the tough times. You've got to keep your business going no matter what. You don't have the luxury of just doing one or the other. The following key strategies will help you stay motivated when it's the hardest, and they will allow you to stay in the zone so you can get the most important things done in your life and business.

The first thing to do is to make sure you're clear on your vision: Clarify the most important things and determine where you are going. From that big vision, break it down to your goal for the year. I know what I'm telling you is simple, but I'm going to ask you to check to see if you have certainty about your big and little goals.

What is key is breaking down that big, often ambiguous, year goal to a 90-day target. It's at this point that people usually struggle when they need to get even more granular and figure out what are the two actions or tasks they need to do every day. It's easy to have a one-year goal. We may even have a clear 90-day goal, but most people lack clarity on the most important things they need to do each day to make sure they stay on track to hit that 90-day goal.

Another successful strategy for your business is to make sure you're planning your week. If you fail to plan your week, you're literally planning to fail your week. Are you with me? On Sunday night sit down and determine what your week is going to look like, and the most important things that you will need to get done. Make sure you include these items in your schedule.

Do the Sunday night review for an epic life. Ask yourself the weekly questions, write down the answers, and schedule your calendar for the week. Does your calendar match your goals? Write down your 3 MUSTS, the three most important things you must get done that week.

If you're struggling with some or all aspects of your life, it may be hard nail an entire day down. I had one gentleman get clear on the most important things he needed to do in the morning, and then give himself permission that while he was in such a turbulent phase, he could just nail those several things in the morning and let the rest of the day happen. Everything else would line up.

In your business, get clear on where you're going. Break it down to that 90-day goal, and then break that down even further by identifying the two or three things you've got to do every single day to make sure you're on track. That way, if all heck breaks loose at least you've got what you've planned done.

Another useful practice is to write down the three or four reasons why you're going to push through, why you're not going to give up, and why following through is so critical to you. Anticipate your possible hold-ups and mentally prepare for them.

Next, let's talk about your relationships. When you go through tough times, sometimes the people who suffer are the people closest to you. We know that people who are suffering often hurt other people. If we're in turmoil, if we're battered, we can damage the people closest to us. We can isolate ourselves and neglect our most important relationships. Especially, in our marriages, or a close partner relationship.

You've got to pre-plan, *How am I going to take care of this relationship?* Here's what's underneath: *How do I check myself before I wreck myself? What are the things I can do to take care of my relationship before it gets weird?*

Great relationships don't happen overnight. They take work. They require effort. One of the things I've begun to realize in my own business is how much time I've spent getting better at my business. I would go to seminars; I would plan my week. I would practice scripts. I would strive in many different ways to be incredible, to be epic in my business life. But it hit me one day. I asked myself: *How much time, effort and planning am I putting into my relationships?* I spent hours getting ready for one conversation with a client, but I didn't spend any time getting ready for a more critical conversation with my spouse.

This won't apply to all of you, but let's spend a little time exploring the marriage relationship. I'm sure those of you who aren't married might be able to get something out of it as well.

I'm going to ask you to remember what it was like at the beginning for your relationship. At the beginning of an attachment, when we first start dating, we're kind of far away from each other. The more we get to know each other, the closer and closer and closer we get until all of a sudden, it's just bliss. Then we get married, and everything's fireworks. The eye-opening piece is that for some people in relationships the wedding was and will remain the closest moment they have. Because if you're not careful, what will happen? You will begin to drift away.

Most people don't choose a relationship to end overnight. But how many times have you heard: "I don't even know what happened in our marriage; it just ended." Well, if we're not intentional, we drift. Ask yourself: *How do I intentionally take care of my relationships so that things don't get off kilter?* One of the reasons you change the oil in your car is, so you don't have a big, costly repair down the road. We need to do those same kinds of preventative maintenance on our relationships.

Here are some of the things that you can do to take care of your relationship. First off, start dating again. When you were dating your spouse, you were playing all in. You let a whole lot of irritations go. If you came home and there were socks on the floor, it was not a big deal because they were your person, the most amazing person in the world, and everything was great. But later on that stuff becomes a big deal. What I'm going to ask you to do is contemplate dating your spouse again.

Second, set up a weekly check in with your spouse. I mentioned this concept earlier in the book, but I want you to see it played out. Every Sunday night my wife and I sit down and I ask her five meaningful questions. I say, "What was great this week? What was the thing this last week that made you the happiest?" I ask her, "What's one thing that I'm doing you want me never to stop doing?" Then I ask her, "What's one thing I'm doing that you would love for me to stop doing?" The final question is, "How are we doing on a scale from one to 10; where are we?" If my wife says, "We're a seven," I go, "Awesome, what would it take..." I don't go for a 10, I say, "What would it take to move us up one or two notches? What would it take for us to be an eight or a nine?" Usually she'll give me a solid answer.

After that, I ask, because it's significant to her, "What's the one thing that I could do this week to best support you? What's the one thing I could do for you?" That check-in is so critical. It's mind-blowing how many people drift apart and they're not even aware that they're drifting apart. Set up this stuff before you need it.

Next, make sure you have some common goals. Relationships are either about problems or they're about goals. Your relationship is probably focused on either all the problems, or it's focused on where you're going. I think your business is perhaps the same way, yet this dynamic really shows up in our relationships. Are you focused on problems or are you focused on goals? You've got to be intentional about having common goals. That doesn't mean all your goals are exactly the same. It demonstrates you're supporting each other in your goals and you know what they are. Do you know the goals of the people closest to you?

Here's the next thing you can do to keep your relationship in a healthy state. One of the quality books I read years ago is *The Five Love Languages*. It talks about how every person receives love differently. Some people feel loved when they are physically touched; some people need time, and some rely on words of affirmation. Get that book, read it, and discover how the people in your life feel loved.

My wife and I are very different; we feel love in different ways. I'm a "words of affirmation and physical touch" kind of guy, and she's a "time and acts of service" gal. I've got to love her in the way that makes her feel loved. The golden rule is to treat people how you want to be treated. But, the platinum rule is to treat people how *they* want to be treated. Find out how the people in your life feel loved, how they experience love, and love them in that way.

Another tactic on how to keep your marriage tight, which I heard from Tony Robbins years ago, is to do some love flooding every once in a while. Love flooding is when you sit down with the significant person in your life, and say, "You know what? I'm just going to tell you all the things I love about you. It's going to feel weird, but I'm going to tell you I love that you get up early in the morning. I love that you prepare for your day. I love that you smile when I walk in the door. I love how you are with your friends." Just pour gratitude and love upon them and share with them all the great things you love about them every once in a while.

It's weird and awesome, so go do it. None of us do this enough. Write some notes; have some fun with it. Are you having fun in your relationship? Don't forget that part.

The final tactic on marriage is to be purposeful about how you're going to take care of your relationships in tough times. If you start doing it now, you can avoid the dicey times moving forward.

TIP: If you want to go deeper into having epic relationships with other humans and improve your marriage, I highly recommend the book *Starved Stuff* by Matt Townsend. I have read almost every marriage book out there and this one is by far the best.

Another relationship which applies to many, but not all, is that of a parent. There are reams of information on the internet and in print about how to be a good parent. But I think the most crucial piece is time and attention.

To keep these crucial parent-child relationships healthy, you need to carve hours out of your schedule when your kids are your only focus. Schedule this time. Don't answer the phone, don't peruse the internet, focus on them, and something that interests them. My current favorite is lego time, but that will change as they mature. Create special things that you do together whether it is sporting events, visiting ice cream parlors, or researching cars. What is important is you make memories. Frequently, no matter their age, let the child lead in regards to how you spend your time. But also jump in with something impromptu, like a visit to a racetrack, a cooking class for kids, or a ride on a scooter. You will never regret spending time with your kids.

Now, let's talk about how you are going to take care of your body. You've got one place to live and this is it. If you don't take care of this house, you are in trouble. How are you going to be physically healthy? It's interesting that people begin to neglect their body when they go through tough times.

When people come to me and share, "I'm struggling with motivation. I'm struggling to work," one of the first things that a coach taught me years ago was to ask was, "How are you sleeping? How are you eating? Are you having any fun?" If you're not taking care of your body, you're not going to feel like you can dominate at work because your lack of energy will pull you back.

One of the obvious ways we struggle with depression is when we neglect our health. When your body feels terrible, you feel terrible. It starts with your morning routine. *How do I get up in the morning? Am I excited about the morning? Am I planning my day?* Get up, go for a walk. One of the most important actions you can take when you first wake up is to drink a bunch of water, just hydrate the hell out of your body. Too many of us hit coffee all day long. Hydrate. It's incredible that when you begin to take care of your body, every other area in your life gets better as well.

Ask yourself, *What am I eating? Am I putting good food in my body? Am I drinking enough water? Am I exercising my body? Am I having sex?* Yep, I said it. Sex is important, and you know it.

An object that's moving usually continues to move. An object at rest usually continues to stay at rest. Your body's the same way. Continue to move your body, go exercise, go outside. I tell my clients to plan to take a little walk and get some fresh air throughout the day. Ask yourself specific questions about your daily activities. You've only got one body.

The last area that you've got to pre-plan is your time. Your time is incredibly precious, and you're not making any more of it, correct? Time is the enemy sometimes because it marches on no matter what you do. I'm going to give you a couple of approaches to handle your time at a really high level.

The first one is that you must understand time management is BS. What I mean by that is it's not about "time management," it's about "priority management." You have to make sure the most important things show up first, that the crucial and valuable action items are included in your day. Most people are busy, busy, busy. The question is, *Am I getting the most important tasks done?* First, question: Do you know what those most important things are?

A friend gave me a quote: "The things that are the most important rarely scream the loudest." The reality is, you run your day, or your day runs you. Are you clear on the items that are critical to complete? It was Alfred A. Montapert who said, "Do not confuse motion and progress. A rocking horse keeps moving but does not make any progress."

Are you clear on the most important jobs you need to finish so you can make progress? One task real estate agents need to ensure is done every day is to work on their lead generation for new clients. When I work with real estate agents, I say, "Imagine that every day you come into your office and in the corner is a little frog named Timmy. Timmy represents your lead generation. Your task for the day is to take care of Timmy. Watch him, feed him, check his water. Whatever Timmy needs, you've got to take care of that frog."

I go on to explain, "If you ignore it, here's what will happen. Every hour you ignore the most critical item on your list, (your lead generation if you're in real estate), Timmy doubles in size. You go and get a cup of coffee, come back and Timmy has doubled in size. Then you think, *I can avoid doing what I need to do a little longer,* so you go to lunch, and then you come back. Now Timmy has quadrupled in size and changed his name to Killer. He's just standing there with three tattoos, looking at you eyeball-to-eyeball.

Isn't that what it feels like when we ignore our top priorities? They get bigger and bigger and bigger. If I don't take care of it and go home, then I'm going home with guilt because I know I left Timmy/Killer in the office. I've got to take care of the most important to-dos every single day.

Now, the cool thing is when I do take care of the important stuff, especially in the morning, I have a renewed sense of joy and confidence because I did it. The added benefit is I don't have to hang out with "Killer."

Let me share two more priority-management words of wisdom: Remove distractions and do one task at a time. In a study done a couple of years ago, we learned 24 percent of your work day is lost between distractions and switching back and forth between tasks. That 24 percent of your day is wasted because you didn't do one focused chore at a time. That means for every week; you could literally take a day off and get the same amount of stuff done if you were focused. Often, it's just a matter of getting better at what you're doing, implementing a new strategy to get more done in the same amount of time.

The most successful people I know don't have any more time in the day than anybody else, yet they get more done because they've implemented successful strategies. They've planned their day, and they do what's most important in the morning. They have high energy because they're taking care of their body. They have effective processes to get their checklists done. These are the people who live big lives; who can go home at the end of the day proud of who they are and what they've accomplished.

Taking care of yourself means pre-planning to handle failure. You have a spare tire underneath your car in case you get a tire. You have a first-aid kit in your house in case you or someone else gets hurt. You have a hide-a-key by your front door in case you lock yourself out.

I want you to go through these five areas: your mind, your business, your relationships, your body and your time. Pre-plan how you're going to take care of these areas of your life, especially when it's harder than usual. Now, take it one step further and ask yourself, *What are the things I need to begin doing now to check myself before I wreck myself? What are the things I can do to maintain my body now before it's too late? What are the things I can do to keep a consistently strong relationship now before we drift?* Apply these questions to all the five aspects of your life that require your pre-planning.

If you're going bowling with your child, you put the bumpers up before you throw the bowling ball. You wouldn't watch the child throw the bowling ball, then freak out in the middle and yell, "Where are the bumpers?"

These tactics that we're talking about are just like putting bumpers up in your life. They keep you from drifting too far to one side or the other. They protect you from getting to a place where recovery is really, really hard. Put the bumpers up; write down these tactics. Plan, in all five of these critical categories, how you are going to take care of yourself before it's too late. Do the work, write your plan down, and I will see you in step nine.

STEP 9

Soul Pain Creates a Gift for Others

"One day, in retrospect, the years of struggle will strike you as the most beautiful."
-Sigmund Freud

Congratulations, you made it to step nine! You've gone through all these incredible steps. Here's what I love about this The Art of Getting Back Up: it's about you being prepared for rough times. It's about you not ignoring rough times. It's about knowing, *Hey, if rough times happen, here is what I can do to get back up. Here's what I'm going to do to take care of myself and recover as quickly as possible.*

A little while ago I read an interview with Robert Herjavec, one of the sharks on *Shark Tank*. He talked about a time in his life where he felt like he hit rock bottom. Several years ago his marriage ended. He had been married for a long time, over 20 years, had some beautiful children. But when the dissolution happened it caused tension in other relationships, especially with his kids. He talked about how it was incredibly painful to him. As a result, he went to a place that was very dark and he didn't know how to get out of it.

Like so many people, once he was in the dark place, he didn't know what to do, but a friend of his who was a pastor invited him to come volunteer at a homeless shelter for a couple of weeks. Robert said, "What was amazing and wonderful was that nobody knew me, and I was able to just serve."

He helped people with meals, to get clothes and assisted in other ways for several weeks. He had several ah-ha's while serving. He realized that first off, what he perceived to be his rock bottom was where other people were aspiring to get to. Other people would look at him like, "How do *I* get there? That sounds awesome!" The whole experience gave him a keen awareness and a new perspective. This is what he used to pull himself out of his trenches.

His rock bottom was not as bad as he thought. His rock bottom was a place that other people were seeking. People who, he began to realize, had major battles going on in their lives. Another thing that blew him away was how some of these people were happier and more joyful than he was. He began to spend time with them, and their joy, happiness, appreciation, and gratitude wore off on him. He was proud to say later on, "I didn't help them. They helped me. Those people saved my life."

Step nine is about giving back.

Something miraculous happens when you stop just looking inward, focusing on all of your stuff, and instead you give back and focus on helping other people. It is magic what takes place when you stop obsessing about your day-to-day details, and you try to help other people with their problems and agonies. I'm going to challenge you to pre-plan how you're going to give back during tough times.

You should start giving back right now. Yes, right now. Create a strategy in your life to give back. When you do this, it helps give you perspective. It helps bring you joy. It pulls you out of the Storm. Go volunteer at a hospital. Go spend some time with people who are stuck in a sick room. If you've ever been in a hospital alone, feeling trapped, it's so heart-lifting to have someone come in and talk to you. You can read books to some of the kids who can't leave. Hold the hand of an elderly patient who is alone.

Go volunteer at a nursing home. Get a group of people to go pick up trash on the side of the highway. Volunteer at a youth center. There are so many meaningful ways that you can give back. Deliver food to people who are homebound. I guarantee that when you give gratitude, when you give back, it's almost impossible to stay in a negative state.

One of the little strategies that I use on a daily basis is, if I'm struggling, I'll pick up the phone and call two or three people. I'll give them gratitude because I know that when I give gratitude, it will immediately pull me out of my negative state.

Choose some of these little tips to get out of a negative state, to give back in substantial way, and to step into who you truly are.

One of the things that helped me as I was going through my tough time was realizing that what I was going through, was going to help other people. I was going to be able to give back what I'd learned and experienced. A counselor of mine said once, "Usually, the people that God uses the most, the people that impact the world at the highest level, are the most wounded."

It helped me to recognize that if I could get through my stuff, I would be able to give what I had received back. I could help other people through their traumas. Years ago, when I was in that darkest place, and I was getting ready to take my own life, what I realized was I had always judged other people. Especially people that I had known who had committed suicide. I had believed they were selfish, and I had been puzzled when I thought about them and their decision. *Why would someone ever do that?*

Yet, when I was at my darkest place I felt the same despair and understood what they must have gone through. Now, when someone comes to me and says, "I'm struggling with depression or suicide," I understand where they're at. Because of what I went through, I can help on a whole new level where some other people aren't able to help. When you experience soul pain, there's a gift in there somewhere.

You only receive that particular gift by going through your pain. When you come out of it, you can help other people and begin to change the world. But you've got to go through it to receive the gift.

This is a short chapter, but that is because I want you to write it yourself. Create the content by going out and fitting in where you can make a difference. Choose to spend time helping those you see around you who need help. In turn you will be lifted up at the same time.

The Art of Getting Back Up

Sometimes we fall down in little ways, and sometimes we take a big giant flop of failure. This happens to everybody, but the outcome is different when you understand the art of getting back up again.

I'm going to challenge you to apply the nine steps that I have just shared with you to your life. Make them your own. Write them out so you are ready to go. Write out the questions you're going to ask yourself. Write out the ways you're going to give back.

These nine steps really come down to the awareness that sometimes you will struggle. As you've heard, "winter is coming," and the reality is a Storm is coming. Life is unfair, and my guess is, a challenging event is going to happen to you sooner or later. Whether you're in a tough time as you read this, or your problems develop in your future, these steps empower you to get up now. More importantly, you can use them to pre-plan for a future Storm. This preparation is about you collecting the tools and strategies for yourself now, so you can go through the Storm in an effective and progressive way.

I am thrilled that you've been with me on this journey. I'm so grateful I was able to share so much with you. I've been working on this book for years because I believe that so many of us are using tactics, but we haven't unleashed the power within them. Instead, we usually just piece together how we will get back up as we are in the moment. But I believe it's incredibly powerful when you have a roadmap in front of you.

So, let's review the nine steps. Organize in your mind how these fit you, and then lay the groundwork for your plan.

The First Step on the journey to recovery is to know when to stop. Stop going in the wrong direction, stop hurting yourself or your business. Stop and grab the tool you need to put out the fire.

You will then need to plan how to get real about your situation. The Second Step helps you to determine where you are at and recognize your new normal. Then you can make decisions based on that reality.

In the Third Step, you have to force yourself to choose what road to take. Do you want to remain in the victim cul-de-sac? Or do you want to go somewhere? Choose your direction.

In Step Four we discussed how you need to take the time to feel and acknowledge the pain or injury you have suffered. You must treat injuries, heal and forgive yourself or others before you can move on.

In Step Five you learned how to ask questions. Clear-cut, straightforward questions, which get to the root of your problems, and point to where you want to go.

You discovered some tools to exercise that "decision muscle" in Step Six. Understanding that sometimes you just have to make a choice so that you can move ahead.

In Step Seven you were reminded that you are not alone. You realized that everybody goes through tough times, depression and more. And then I pointed out that you need to surround yourself with friends who will lift you up and encourage you. Don't forget to maintain brave relationships.

Pre-planning for pitfalls by creating a first-aid kit to meet future needs is discussed in Step Eight where you will organize plans to take care of the five important areas of your life.

And the final step, Step Nine, is taking what you have learned and sharing it with others. Helping those who are suffering and in pain. People who need empathy, not pity. In making the time to help them, you will lift them up and feed your own soul at the same time.

All these steps together allow you to grab your first-aid kit, prepare your hide-a-key, and overcome your hurdles in a powerful way. You are able to move forward much faster when you write down your plan rather than just attempting to keep it in your mind. Personally, I even put a little fake hide-a-key on the side of my desk. It reminds me that I'm going to be okay. It reminds me, that if I fall down, I know how to get back up.

SUMMARY

Thank you so much for going all in.

Thank you for allowing me to spend time with you. I would love for you to send me your feedback. Please share which chapter or section of this book stood out for you. What are some of the questions you asked yourself that were incredibly powerful? Maybe you added your own stuff, maybe you took some away?

In whatever way you were able to move through the process, I would love to hear what you've pushed through and how these nine steps have helped you.

Wayne@WayneSalmans.com

My one request would be to share this book with somebody else. Share this with someone the steps that have been effective and have impacted you. The mission of Hero Nation, which I believe with all my heart, is that if you want to help other people you first have to help yourself. It's just like when you're on a plane, and the flight attendants tell you to put your mask on first. I believe that you've got to be your own hero before you can be the hero for other people.

The Art of Getting Back Up is about empowering and equipping you with the tools you need to be your own hero so you can go on to be the hero for others.

Watch the entire video series for free:

www.TheArtofGettingBackUp.com

All right my friends. I love you. I appreciate you. I will see you down the road.

Be your own hero.

Continue the journey with me and a community of world changers at **www.TheHeroNation.com.**

WHAT'S NEXT

The Hero Nation Coaching Company provides several opportunities for you to work with Wayne Salmans.

Hero Nation is a mastermind & training community for big-dreaming achievers. If you are a business leader looking to make more than $250K per year without sacrificing family, health or dreams, consider this your tribe. Gain momentum, clarity, discover powerful tactics, implement systems, tap into massive momentum, gain higher & more predictable paychecks and balance it with a BIG, EPIC life. We've done it. You can too.

Visit the Hero Nation at www.TheHeroNation.com for more information on:
- Fuel Hybrid Coaching Program
- The TRIBE, 1-1 Coaching with Wayne
- Have Wayne Keynote Your Next Event

Gift for You

**Book a Free Strategy Session with a
Certified Hero Nation Coach.**

www.theHeroNation.com/p/free-strategy-session

Made in the USA
Columbia, SC
24 October 2018